CW00742201

The Loyal Lusitanian Legion During the Peninsular War

SIR ROBERT WILSON

The Loyal Lusitanian Legion During the Peninsular War

The Campaigns of Wellington's Portuguese Troops
1809-11

John Scott Lillie and William Mayne

LEONAUR

The Loyal Lusitanian Legion During the Peninsular War
The Campaigns of Wellington's Portuguese Troops 1809-11
by John Scott Lillie and William Mayne

First published under the title
A Narrative of the Campaigns of the Loyal Lusitanian Legion

Leonaur is an imprint of Oakpast Ltd

Copyright in this form © 2014 Oakpast Ltd

ISBN: 978-1-78282-367-4 (hardcover)
ISBN: 978-1-78282-368-1 (softcover)

http://www.leonaur.com

Publisher's Notes

The views expressed in this book are not necessarily
those of the publisher.

Contents

DEDICATION
TO THE
BRITISH AND PORTUGUESE OFFICERS
IN THE
SERVICE OF THE PRINCE REGENT OF PORTUGAL

The author (an officer in His Majesty's service, and a captain in the Portuguese) had intended to ask permission to inscribe this small treatise to the Right Honourable Lord Viscount Castlereagh, under whose auspices the Loyal Lusitanian Legion was raised; who assisted its establishment, and encouraged its endeavours; and to whom the British officers who were attached to it may still look for protection.

But to avoid the suspicion of flattery or presumption, he dedicates it to his brethren in arms, assured from his knowledge of His Lordship's character, that he will participate with more pleasure in any observations on their worth and excellent conduct than in the most studied panegyrics on his own.

Advertisement

Having published certain documents referring to circumstances connected with the important campaigns of that late distinguished corps the Loyal Lusitanian Legion, which were given merely as hints to satisfy the inquisitive partiality of my friends; and many persons, chiefly military men, who had expected to find a more perfect detail, having been disappointed in the perusal,—I am now induced, by their request, and to gratify their wishes, to lay before the public a more enlarged account of a corps which is now no more, having, too unfortunately for its own existence, during the early stages of the war upon the Peninsula, created a jealousy in a quarter which, aided by power and intrigue, caused alterations the most prejudicial to its interests, and ultimately succeeded in effecting its dissolution.

And even in extinguishing its name; no less to the mortification and regret of the British officers who, under every inconvenience and difficulty, had embarked in this cause, and who, under Lord Castlereagh, were the means of its origin, than to the Portuguese, who also had so zealously assisted in its formation. Nor was its extinction less painfully felt by the patriots of the Peninsula, who were well acquainted with its services, and to whom it will be a proud satisfaction to reflect that its fame still lives, and that Spain, Portugal, and the enemy to whom it was opposed, will do equal justice to its reputation.

To the real advantage of its services I believe I may confidently appeal to those very respectable authorities Sir John Cradock, then commander-in-chief, Mr. Frere, and Mr. Villiers, His Majesty's ministers in Spain and Portugal; and may venture to state that, besides the defence of Castille, Almeida, Ciudad Roderigo, and their valuable magazines, the safety of Seville, the seat of government (and power, almost at an end from the successes of the enemy) was secured and protected by the operations and perseverance of this Legion alone, which great benefit has since been officially acknowledged by the government of Spain:

> That General Cuesta being thus permitted to assemble the fugitives of Castanos's army at Badajos, was enabled to save his country at that epoch by covering Andalusia, and fighting the Battle of Medellen, which checked Marshal Victor, and obliged 15,000 men to march from Salamanca into Estremadura:

> That the non-embarkation of the British Army at Lisbon, under General Sir John Cradock, is to be ascribed to the resolute conduct of this corps:

> That General Lapisse was thus opposed in his descent of the Douro and junction with Marshal Soult at Oporto, who was obliged to remain there until Sir Arthur Wellesley's arrival with reinforcements in Portugal.

These facts are all on record, and the enemy's statements and dispatches sufficiently confirm them, undeniably proving the value and importance of the services of this corps, and the support its perseverance afforded to the combined armies. The patriot Portuguese officers of this Legion equally shared with the British in the endurance of every hardship, and in every trial of danger and skill; nor were the men less exemplary for a patience, an alacrity, a zeal, and a courage, well worthy of the highest admiration; and these great qualities were thus honourably displayed both by officers and men at a moment when all was doubt and difficulty, despondency or despair; when every struggle seemed the last, and the enemy, unresisted or irresistible, appeared to spread conquest and destruction over all.

The following detail of the services of this corps will, I trust, prove interesting; and I must confess myself indebted to a young officer, one of the most meritorious *flowers*[1] of the corps, for this well arranged narrative, and for his permission to introduce into it some remarks and observations that I had an opportunity of making while I was colonel-commandant of the first battalion, and second in command in this service; but I have confined this merely to a part of my own journal, in Appendix I, containing official letters and communications copied from originals in my possession, which appeared to me necessary to corroborate circumstances, or to which reference may have been made in the narrative.

1. Captain Lillie of the 60th British Infantry and lieut.-colonel in the Portuguese Legion

I cannot take leave of my subject without one observation, which, extraordinary as it may appear, is nevertheless strictly true. I mention it with much pain, and in the hope that it may yet be remedied, that (with the exception of Sir Robert Wilson) none of the British officers who organised this first Portuguese corps, have derived any advantage whatever from the British Government, while those who were attached to it, in the second instance, at a later period, and in securer times, under Sir William Beresford, have been advanced by repeated steps of promotion: For instance, officers who left this country as captains, being now lieutenant-colonels in His Majesty's service, and colonels and brigadier-generals in the Portuguese.

An additional motive for aiding this slight memorial of the Loyal Lusitanian Legion, and this young officer's humble, but honest testimony to its value and services, is a disposition (I regret to say) that has ever been too apparent on the part of the officers now serving in the Peninsula to under-rate the utility and importance of this corps, which I am persuaded has arisen solely from want of information, and, which I flatter myself this relation will effectually remove.

William Mayne,
Knight of the Military Order of Alcantara,
Colonel in the Service of the
Prince Regent of Portugal,
And late Lieutenant-Colonel of the
1st Battalion of the Loyal Lusitanian Legion.

Park-street, Grosvenor-square,
June 4, 1812.

Introductory Chapter from Colonel Mayne's Journal in 1808

The name of Portugal is of recent origin. In the Roman period there was a town called Calle, (now Oporto,) near the mouth of the Douro, and the haven being eminently distinguished, the barbarism of the middle ages conferred on the circumjacent region the name of Port Calle, which as the country was gradually recovered from the Moors, was yet more improperly extended to the whole kingdom: the ancient name was Lusitania, but the boundaries do not exactly correspond.

Portugal extends about 360 British miles in length, by 140 in breadth, and is supposed to contain 32,000 square miles, which, with a population of 1,838,879, will yield 67 inhabitants to the square mile. By another calculation it is computed that Portugal contains 2740 Portuguese leagues of 17 to a degree. Guthrie places Portugal between 37° and 42° north, and 7° and 1° west. The extent and population thus approach nearly to those of Scotland; but by some accounts the population of Portugal may exceed the calculation here followed by nearly half a million.

The original population of Portugal may be traced in that of Spain, and has undergone the same revolutions. See the work of the learned Portuguese antiquary Resende, *Antiquitates Lusitaniae.*

The progressive geography of Portugal is also included in that of Spain, till the 11th century, when it began to form a separate state. The kings of Castile had recovered a small part of the country from the Moors about the year 1050, and the conquest was gradually extended from the north till about the middle of the 13th century, when the acquisition of Algarva completed the present boundaries of Portugal.

The historical epochs of so recent a date cannot be numerous, nor is it necessary to recur to those ancient events which more regularly belong to the history of Spain.

1st. The kings of Asturias having subdued some of the Moorish chiefs of the north of Portugal, Alphonso the Great established Episcopal sees in the part between the Entre Douro e Minho. In 1054 King Ferdinand of Castile extended his conquests to Coimbra; and on sharing his dominions amongst his sons, Don Garcia, along with Gallicia, had a part of Portugal, whence he is styled on his tomb *Rex Portugaliae et Galliciae*.

2nd. Alphonso VI. brother to Garcia, and King of Castile, having favourably admitted several French princes to his court, among them was Henry, whom he nominated Count of Portugal, giving him his natural daughter Theresa in marriage. This Henry was the grandson of Robert, Duke of Burgundy, son of Robert, King of France; the Spanish, however, derive him from the House of Lorrain.

Henry appears as Count of Portugal, and he obtained many victories over the Moors, and died in 1112, leaving a son, Alphonso the First. In the year 1139, Alphonso I. gained an illustrious victory over five Moorish princes, and was proclaimed king on the field of battle. In 1148, he seized Lisbon, by the assistance of a fleet of crusaders going to the Holy Land. Alphonso died in 1185, aged 94. Such are the foundations of the Portuguese monarchy.

3rd. Alphonso the Third, about the year 1254, completed the conquest of Algarva. Portugal continued to be fortunate in a succession of great princes; but the wars against the Moors were unhappily followed by those against the King of Castile, which have implanted such a deep hatred between the nations.

4th. Portugal was to attract the attention of Europe by her commercial discoveries. In 1415, John the Great, King of Portugal, carried his arms into Africa, captured Ceuta, and in 1420 Madeira. In 1402 he took the Canaries, and assumed the title of king of those islands. The Portuguese discoveries proceeded under John's successors, Edward and Alphonso V. and the auspices of Prince Henry, till in the reign of John II. they extended to the Cape of Good Hope, and in that of Emanuel, Vasco de Gama opened a way to the West Indies.

5th. John the Third admitted the Inquisition in 1525, since which event the Portuguese monarchy has rapidly declined.

6th. Sebastian, King of Portugal, landed a large army in Africa, and was slain in battle. He was succeeded by his uncle, called Henry, who dying two years afterwards, Portugal was seized by Philip the Second, King of Spain, in 1530.

7th. By the Revolution of 1640, the House of Braganza was placed on the throne of Portugal. John the Fourth was a descendant of the ancient royal family by the female line. Little of consequence has since arisen, except the earthquake in Lisbon in 1755. The celebrated administration of Pombal, and the recent intermarriages with Spain, which did promise, at no remote period, to unite the kingdoms, deserve also to be noticed. The last peace with Spain seems to have been procured on humiliating terms.

The antiquities chiefly consist in Roman monuments, with a few Moorish remains. At Evora are well preserved ruins of a temple of Diana, and an aqueduct ascribed to the celebrated Quintilius Sertorius *(Life by Plutarch)*. At Chaves there is a Roman bridge, erected in the time of the Roman Emperor Trajan, which is still entire.

Among the antiquities of the middle ages is the noble monastery of Batalha, in Portuguese Estremadura, sixty miles north of Lisbon, formed by John the First, at the close of the 14th century, in consequence of a great victory over the King of Castile (one of the most noble monuments of what is called the Gothic style of architecture.)

The religion of Portugal is the Roman Catholic, and a strict observance of its duties forms one of the national characteristics, the men vying with the women in attention to their repeated daily devotions. A patriarch, who does not seem to possess any great power, is at the head of the Portuguese church.

Convents for males	417
Ditto for women	150
Secular clergy	22,000
Monks	14,000
Nuns	10,000

In Portugal there are 4000 parishes! while in Scotland, of nearly the same extent, there are only 1000; but the Catholic religion affords supplies to a far greater number of priests than the Protestant.

The constitution of Portugal is a monarchy absolute and hereditary; yet in case of the king's decease without issue (male), he is succeeded by his next brother, whose sons have, however, no right to the throne until it has been confirmed by the states. The Prince of Brazil was appointed regent by his mother, the heiress to the kingdom. Don Pedro, his father, was king, as husband to Maria, or, according to the Scottish expression, had the crown matrimonial, but was not regarded as sovereign.

The administration is vested in four ministers of state, with their secretaries. One is president of the treasury, another minister of the interior; a third of war and foreign affairs, and the fourth of the increase of colonies.

In 1796, a great council was established of thirteen members, including the four ministers: they assemble only on solemn occasions: the chancellor is a subordinate officer, and does not administer justice. The chancellor of the court called Rellaçaen, somewhat resembling the Parliament at Paris, is called Regent of the Justices; but the other high courts do not depend on him. There are five councils, which judge without appeal; two for Europe, at Lisbon and Oporto; two for Brazil, at Bahia and Rio Janeiro; and one for Africa, at Goa. By an edict of 4th August, 1769, no laws have positive authority, except the ordinances of the king; but the Roman law maybe consulted as written justice or equity.

The chief articles of the constitution are contained in the statutes of Lamago, founded by Alphonso the First, in 1165. The king's titles are numerous; that of the heir apparent is Prince of Brazil; his eldest son that of Prince of Beira. The laws have few particularities; they are lenient in case of theft, which must be repeated four times before death be the punishment.

An adulteress is condemned to the flames; but this is never put in execution. [1]

There are seven councils—

1. Of the palace, which is supreme in justice, and has all the powers of a Lord Chancellor.

2. The Inquisition, which was declared royal by Joseph; while before it was only papal. It has four inferior chambers, Lisbon, Evora, Coimbra and Goa,

3. Finances.

4. Colonies.

---

1. In England, an adulteress is divorced or separated, and then *legally* permitted to live with her paramour or adulterer!!! So much for the interpretation of the Law of God in different countries.

5. That of honour, or the affairs of the knights.

6. Of war.

7. The Admiralty.

There are five sovereign courts of justice, (Rellaçaen), at Lisbon, Oporto, Bahia, Rio Janeiro, and Goa.

Portugal is divided into six provinces:—

1. Entre Douro e Minho.—2. Tras os Montes.—3. Beira.—4. Estremadura.—5. Alentejo.—6. Algarva.

The two first are in the north of the kingdom.

The two second in the middle, and the two last in the south.

The first province derives its name from its situation between the two rivers, and is very populous and fertile.

The second is mountainous, as the name implies; but there are vales which contain vineyards, and other cultivated lands. Beira is a large and fertile province, and is rivalled in soil by Estremadura, which like the Spanish province of the same name, is said to derive its etymology from having been an extensive frontier to the sea against the Moors.

The Alentejo having been most exposed to the attacks of the Spaniards, is defective in population.

Algarva is a very small division, which has, however, the honour of forming an addition to the royal titles, as Navarre to that of France, those lesser provinces having been comparatively recent acquisitions. The population of the whole is, according:

| To Boeticher | 1,838,879 |
| To Murphy | 2,588,470 |

As this last is derived from Portuguese authors, having little skill in statistics, it seems to be exaggerated.

The chief colony of Portugal is that established in Brazil; and she still retains many settlements in Africa, with Goa and Macao in the East Indies, the relics of great power and territory.

The army is computed at only 24,000, and the militia at an equal number, forming a very respectable numerical force upon paper.

The naval power, once so considerable, is now reduced to thirteen sail of the line, and fifteen frigates; and as is the maritime system reduced, so is the formation of the army unequal to active campaigns.

Since the year 1763 the soldiers have been well paid. At present there are twenty-eight regiments of infantry, twelve of cavalry, five of artillery, and one of light troops; all strengthened according to circumstances.

There were 43 regiments of the regular militia. The military governments are seven, the six provinces and the government of Oporto composed of a part of Beira, and a part of Entre Douro e Minho.

The revenue is calculated at 2 millions sterling, or at 70,000,000 French *livres*, and the national debt at 100,000,000. The gold of Brazil mostly passes to England in return for articles of industry.

Portugal retains small influence in the political scale of Europe; her commerce is wholly dependent on England; but by land she is exposed to no dangers except from Spain, or by its consent: the union of the two countries would doubtless be advantageous to both.

The cities of Portugal are	23
Villas or municipalities	350
Villages very numerous.	
Parishes no less than	4262

The inhabitants of the northern provinces are esteemed more industrious and sincere than those of the south, who are reckoned more polite and indolent.

In general, the Portuguese are a fine race, with regular features embrowned by the sun, and with dark expressive eyes. The prejudices of nobility are as common in Portugal as in Spain. All ranks seem fond of retirement and silence, and little inclined to bustling scenes; yet they are friendly to strangers, particularly to those of the Roman Catholic persuasion.[2]

The women are of small stature, yet graceful. Like other southern nations the Portuguese esteem a plump roundness of the limbs; nor is the black and brilliant eye without its share of modern admiration. Ladies of rank still work at the distaff, and the oriental custom of sitting at the doors on cushions is often practised. The dress resembles the Spanish; but the men prefer the English, with the exception of the large loose cloak. The peasantry remain miserable vassals of the *fidalgos*, or gentlemen.

The peasants live on salt fish and vegetables. In their diet, the Por-

---

2. Hence probably the great influence which some Irish officers possess at this moment in the allied armies. Would to God, instead of cavilling at home about modes of faith, and resisting Irish emancipation, the cabinet of Great Britain had availed itself of the zeal and promptitude of the Irish Roman Catholics at the commencement of the war in Spain. But we seemed doomed to dispute about a straw, while the beam is ready to fall upon our own heads!

tuguese are abstemious, and the beauty of the climate induces them to live in the open air, the house being merely a convenience to sleep in. The games are billiards, cards and dice. The common people fence with a quarter staff; but their chief delight is in their bull fights.

The arts and sciences are almost entirely neglected, except by a few of the clergy; neither painting nor taste are to be found in Portugal.

The language differs from that of Castile in a greater degree than might be expected from circumstances. As the royal race was of French extraction, it is supposed many of their words are derived from the Limosin and other dialects of the south of France. It is grave and solemn, and would have been but little known to foreigners, but for the fame of the Lusiade.

The commencement of literature may be traced to Decriz, the sixth sovereign, who founded the University of Coimbra, and is said to have written Amadis de Gaul. In late times Saa de Miranda excelled in pastoral poetry. The chief historians are Joao de Barros, Fr. Luis de Souza, Fr. Bernado de Brido vicira, Osorio, Bishop of Sylves, Duarte Ribeiro de Macedo, the venerable Bart, de Quartel, and the Count de Ercheira, Camoens, Digo Bernardes, Antonio Barberza, Bacelar, and Gabriel Peirira.

Dramatic writers are also mentioned. Antonio Josephus who has written four volumes of plays; Nicola Luis, who is called the Portuguese Plautus; and Pedro Nunez, who distinguished himself in the sixteenth century.

Of late years natural history is begun to be studied; but Portugal is the last of nations in that branch. Marquis de Pombal endeavoured to introduce the sciences—since his time they have dwindled, though they never made much progress.

The Royal Academy of Lisbon exists no more, and the University of Evora remains suppressed since 1759.

Education is much neglected in Portugal There are 800 students in the University of Coimbra.

Lisbon, the capital, was called by the ancients Ulyssippo, fabulously ascribed to Ulysses. The situation is grand. On the north side it has the Tajo, sheltered on the N. W. by a ridge of hills. This capital was retaken from the Moors in the 12th century. The population amounts to 200,000. The earthquake in 1755, (a dreadful and memorable epoch among the inhabitants,) has contributed to the beauty of the new city, the new streets being broad and handsome, and well paved. For constant residence the ladies prefer the attic floors, and ventilation and coolness are only consulted, grates being almost unknown, while in winter a warm cloak supplies the place of a fire.

The Patriarchal church is magnificent; and has a revenue of 100,000*l.* The English have an open burial ground, in which are deposited the remains of Fielding. The Royal Monastery of Belem, founded by King Emanuel in 1499, is five miles S.W. of Lisbon, and to the north is a noble modern aqueduct completed in 1732. Consumption of butchers' meat in Lisbon in 1798 was 27,985 oxen, 1,272 calves, 27,562 sheep, and 11,927 hogs.

The northern branch of the Tajo at Lisbon is alone practicable for large vessels.

Oporto is the most considerable town, especially in the eye of strangers; it is seated on the north side of the Douro, five miles from the sea, upon the declivity of a hill; the houses rising like an amphitheatre. The streets are narrow, the houses ill-constructed, and the population amounts to 30,000. The churches are of little note. The British factory is a large neat building. The chief exports are wine, oranges, lemons, and linen cloth to the American colonies.

Setuval, or St. Ubes, is a considerable town, with about 12,000 inhabitants, and a prosperous commerce. The principal trade of this place consists in salt, of which commodity vast quantities are shipped to all countries.

Braga, though inland, is another considerable town.

In the province of Beira is the venerable city of Coimbra, with its ancient university.

Alentejo contains the city of Evora, rather of ancient fame than of modern consequence.

Tavora is the principal town of Algarve, the number of its inhabitants does not exceed 5000.

The chief edifices of Lisbon are the cathedral and the monasteries. The nobility, as in Spain, crowd to the capital, and the country is little decorated with villas. In the mountains of Cintra, the farthest western extremity of Europe, about twenty miles west of Lisbon, is placed a remarkable monastery, 3000 feet above the sea, and a curious bath, with a never-failing spring. On the east of the mountain is a summer place of Moresque architecture. The environs of Lisbon are rich and delightful, supplying most of the fruits and vegetables used in Lisbon; a small vineyard here called Calcavella, produces the Calcavella wine, near which is the aqueduct of Alcantara.

Here are no canals, nor any necessity for them. The sea coast from

W. to S. Rivers running from W. to E.

The manufactures are few: lately cloths, hats, and paper at Lisbon; but the chief manufactories are those of woollen cloth at Covilhao, Portalegre, and Azeitaou. The greatest intercourse is with England; balance in favour of the latter 400,000*l*. and Ireland gains by her exports 63,000*l*. sterling annually. The Falmouth packets bring remittances frequently of bullion, coin, diamonds, and other precious stones.

Besides woollens and hardware, England exports to Portugal large cargoes of salt and dried fish, the last to the amount of 200,000*l*.

The exports of Portugal are chiefly wine, oil, oranges, lemons, figs, sugar, cotton, bark, drugs, and tobacco. She maintains a considerable trade with her colony the Brazils, the inhabitants of which are computed at 900,000.

The articles exported to America are chiefly woollens, linens, stuffs, gold and silver lace, fish dried in Portugal, hams, &c. with glass of a good quality manufactured at Marinha.

Brazil returns gold, silver, precious stones of various descriptions, rice, wheat, maize, sugar, molasses, ornamental timber, and many other articles rather curious than important. The drugs, spices, and articles used in dying must not be omitted.

The trade with the East Indies is inconsiderable, and that with the other European nations scarcely deserves notice: it is chiefly with Holland, Denmark, France, and Germany; some trade is also carried on with the American States. For internal trade, the great fair of Viseu has long been famous.

The grain was formerly supplied from England, from North America, when in her possession, Barbary, and Prussian Poland. Much rice is consumed, being imported from Carolina.

The coin we call a Johannes or Joe, is in the Portuguese tongue *pega*.

The English moidore is the *monduro*, or *mondea de ouro*, (*i. e.* gold coin.)

Brazil supplies 27,000,000 *francs* annually in gold, or little more than a million sterling: since 1780 more than 100 million (*francs*) of merchandise. As it is well known that a great part of the Portuguese gold comes from Sofala, it must not be included under that of Brazil, if it be not remitted to India and China to purchase merchandise in these countries.

The colonies are Brazil, Mozambic, Melinda, Sofala, Cuama, Angola, Benguella, with the isles St. Thome del Principe, Cape Verd, Madeira, Azores. In India, Goa, Dieu, and Macao in China.

The climate at Lisbon is most excellent and salutary; the fair weather is computed at 200 days in the year, and those of settled rain do not exceed eighty; the medical heat about sixty degrees.

The face of the country is generally fertile, notwithstanding its acclivities. In the north corner there rises a cluster of mountains, seemingly connected with the great Spanish chain. The soil, like that of Spain, is generally light, but the agriculture is in a neglected state. Meadowing is little known, except in the N. W. province of Entre Douro e Minho, and many fine vales remain in a state of nature. The rain is violent while it lasts, and produces torrents, which sometimes destroy the crops.

The River Tajo here has a noble stream, and affords a capacious haven from two to nine miles broad.

Among the native streams is the Mondego, which passes by Coimbra.

The Soro runs into the Tajo and the Cadaon, which form the harbour of Setuval.

There are only three lakes to be seen in Portugal: *viz.* the Escura situated on the summit of the mountain of Estrella in Beira, and which is covered with snow during four or five months,—it is noted for a profound vortex. Another deep pool occurs near the village of Sapellos, which is said to have been the shaft of a gold mine worked by the Romans. The lake of Obidos in Estremadura is sometimes open to the sea, and at other times closed with sand. It contains excellent fish.

The mountains in the N. E. seem an unconnected cluster. Nor have the mountains in the kingdom been exactly described; but the Spanish chain to the north of Madrid, called by some the mountains of Idubeda, enters Portugal near the town of Guarda, and pursues its former course to the S. W.

The chain of Arrabeda in Estremadura, seems a branch or continuation of this. It is chiefly calcareous, and affords beautiful marble.

The chain of Toledo appears (as is not unusual with extensive ranges) to subside abruptly before it enters Portugal; but not far from this, in the province of Alentejo, there is a small chain seven leagues long, by two and a half broad, running between the city of Evora and the town of Estremos, which may be regarded as belonging to this Toledo chain.

The Estrella gives rise to the Mondego and two other rivers, and belongs to the first mentioned chain of the mountains of Idubeda.

Monto Junto, the ancient Sageus, is in Estremadura; its verdure affords a rich pasturage, and the breed of horses was formerly celebrated here. These mountains are well described in Link's work. He visited the northern chain of Geriz, that of Maram, and that of Estrella. They are 6000 feet high (the summits) while some of the Spanish may be 8000. They are all of the granite, and appear gigantic to us islanders.

The zoology of Portugal may be regarded as the same with that of Spain, as well as the botany. The horses are however inferior; but the mules are stronger and more hardy. The oxen sometimes equal in size those of Lincolnshire; cows are rare, as the natural pasture is injured by the heat of the climate, and no attention is paid to artificial meadows. The sheep are neglected, and far from numerous; but swine abound, fed with acorns, and Portugal hams are much esteemed.

Mineralogy has been as much neglected as the agriculture. In the two northern provinces are seen immense mines, supposed to have been worked by the Romans, being those of Lusitania mentioned by ancient authors. The mouth of the largest, cut through the solid rock, is one mile and a half in circumference, and upwards of 500 feet deep; at the bottom it measures 2,400 feet, by 1,400; many subterranean passages pierce the mountain, and the whole works are on the grandest scale. Other ancient mines are found in those provinces: one near the mouth of the Tajo; and under the Spaniards a silver mine was worked near Braganza in 1628, which proved very productive.

Tin was found in the northern provinces, and near Miranda formerly pewter.

There are lead mines at Murza, Lamego, and Cago, and the Galina ore is very productive of silver.

Copper is found near Elvas, and in other districts.

Iron mines are neglected (though coal is found in different parts of the kingdom) from a deficiency of fuel. The coal mines of Buarcos supply the royal foundry at Lisbon. This bed of coal is three feet six inches broad, and enlarges according to the depth.

Emery is found near the Douro, and many beautiful marbles abound in this kingdom. The mountain of Goes, and others, produce fine granite, and talc is met with near Oporto.

Amiante is discovered in such quantities, that it has been recommended to the artillery in the form of incombustible paper.

The bismuth of Estrella, pounded and mingled with white clay, has been found to compose excellent porcelain. Fullers' earth occurs near Guimeraens. Portugal also boasts of antimony, magnesia, and arsenic;

and near Castello Branco, are mines of quicksilver. Rubies in Algarve, jacinths in the ruins of Cavado and Belas; beryl, or aqua marine, in the mountain of Estrella. In short, Portugal abounds with minerals of most descriptions, and nothing is wanting but industry and fuel.

Of the mineral waters, the baths of Caldas de Rainha, in Estremadura, are the most celebrated, and the next are those of Chaldes. There are salt and petrifying springs, and others that have only a supposed property given by the superstition of the Portuguese.

Among the natural curiosities is a high, massy cliff, on the north bank of the River Douro, with carved letters or hieroglyphics, stained with vermilion and blue, beneath which is a grotto, supposed to abound with bitumen. Ever-green groves are cultivated on the banks of this river, which are not very common on other rivers in Spain and Portugal.

The chain of mountains in which the Battle of Busaco was fought, is called Arrabeda, and terminates at Mafra. It seems to be a continuation of the Spanish chain which rises north of Madrid, and enters Portugal near the town of Guarda.

Lisbon is situated on the north bank of the Tagus, 18 miles from the rock, on the north extremity of the harbour, as is Cape Espinhel on the south: it extends four miles in length by two in width.

The entrance of the harbour is defended by nature, by a large bank of sand, which is principally divided into two banks called north and south Catchops. Over this sand-bank there are only two channels navigable for ships of any burden, called north and south channels; the former in the direction from the rock S. E. by E. and nearly parallel with the coast, which is low, and offers points at which troops may conveniently land under cover of ships of war.

The other channel, which is directly between the two Catchops, runs N. E. by N. and both channels, forming the two sides of a triangle, meet at a point within a mile of Fort St. Julien. Ships running up either of those channels are therefore exposed to be raked by the guns of this fort, which probably exceed 200 ordnance. It stands upon a little promontory, is built of stone, and its batteries are about forty feet above the level of the sea. It is not overlooked by any land that is near it, though it is less formidable on the land side than towards the river.

Nearly opposite to Fort St. Julien, on an insulated rock, which forms the eastern point of the S. Catchop, is a little fort called the Bugio; it is of no great strength, and from its circular form (being in fact little more than a town, surrounded by a rampart) could bring few guns to bear on any one point, and might soon be silenced by our shipping.

Beyond St Julien, which is ten miles within the rock, the river narrows; but this is compensated by a bold shore and deep water; and ten miles above this fort, at the village of Almada, the river abruptly spreads into a wide bay.

About seven miles from St. Julien, on another little point on the same side of the river, is Belem Castle; but as the passage is here commanded from both sides, it has, without doubt, received additional batteries. At the back of Belem are some high grounds which overlook it. About two miles from Belem Castle,, we came to the western end of the city, where many ships are anchored. Farther on, and within the city, towards its eastern end, stands Fort St. George, on an elevated spot which commands the city. This fort is not capable of containing more than 5000 men: it is supplied with water by an aqueduct which might be easily cut off.

A Narrative, &c., &c.

Portugal[1] having been entered in 1807, by a French army, fell an easy prey to its lawless invaders, in consequence of the disorganized state of its armies, and the sudden and unexpected attack upon its territories. His Royal Highness the Prince Regent had the good fortune to effect his escape to the British fleet then lying off the mouth of the Tagus, an attempt having been made by the enemy to surprise him in Lisbon, and seize on his person.

The entrance of the French troops into Portugal was not known at Lisbon till their advanced guard arrived at Abrantes, for it was never conceived that they would not pursue the course of the Tagus; to *traverse with an army* the *mountains* of Biera in winter, was deemed impossible. His Royal Highness afterwards proceeded with a good many of the nobility (who likewise escaped) to the Brazils, part of His Royal Highness's dominions; and scarcely had the Portuguese fleet left the Tagus, when the French, with their Spanish auxiliaries, appeared on the hills above Lisbon, under the command of General Junot, who had formed resided for several years as ambassador at the court of Portugal. The subsequent monopolization by the enemy of the property of those Portuguese who remained, together with the heavy contributions and oppressive taxes levied on them, induced many to emigrate to England.

Amongst those loyalists who preferred a temporary banishment from their native land to an abject submission to the French yoke, were many officers who had escaped from the hands of the enemy while endeavouring to remove to France the best organised troops

1. The Spanish Governor of Badajoz inquired of the Marquis D'Alorno, commanding at Elvas, if the French Army then marching into Portugal would be received as friends or enemies.

"We are unable," answered the marquis, "to entertain you as friends, or to resist you as enemies."

of the Portuguese Army. These steadfast patriots remained in England under protection of the British Government, until that government had resolved, in 1808, on sending an army from Great Britain to that country (which had been its ancient and faithful ally for a considerable number of years), for its redemption from the rapacious grasp of the Corsican tyrant.

The British had likewise determined on lending their assistance at this period towards the organization of the native Portuguese, to be aided by experienced and select British officers; and for the purpose of ascertaining how far that project might be successful, they had resolved on forming a legion of those loyal Luzitanian emigrants then in England, the shell of which was shortly completed, under the auspices of Viscount Castlereagh, His Excellency the Chevalier de Souza, the Portuguese ambassador in England, and the venerable Bishop of Oporto, now patriarch of Portugal.[2]

Those patriots thus formed into a legion, eagerly embraced the opportunity thus afforded them of returning to their native shores to seek redress for the cruel grievances, and unremitted insults offered to themselves, their families, and their country, by a lawless band of mercenary invaders. They accordingly set sail in August, for Portugal, accompanied by a few select British officers, under the command of Sir Robert Wilson, who was appointed chief of that corps, which was justly nominated the Loyal Luzitanian Legion, the subsequent operations of which, together with its services, it is the object of the present work to endeavour to elucidate.

In the month of September, 1808, these patriots landed at Oporto, [3] where it was concluded most advisable to recruit and complete a corps for active service. In this city they were received with all possible demonstrations of joy by the inhabitants; who uniting with the gallantry of the bordering peasantry, had risen and overpowered the first French garrison, which occupied it in the month of June, and subsequently aided by the natural defences the country afforded north of the River Douro, had attacked and routed a corps of the enemy, under General Loison, who had attempted to march on Oporto.

On his generals endeavouring to cross the River Douro for that purpose, he was defeated by the gallant and hardy peasantry of the northern provinces who had united at Mezon Frio; and the subse-

---

2. *Vide* Appendix A.
3. Oporto is open and unfortified, except two modern forts next the sea, situated on the Douro, which frequently inundates the quays and lower parts of the city.

quent success was such that the enemy were so completely routed as to lose the entire of their baggage, which fell into the hands of those meritorious peasants; in consequence of which the French judged it expedient not to interfere any farther with the north of Portugal, but to confine their ravages to the southern unprotected provinces; from those hardy peasantry the Loyal Lusitanian Legion had been principally recruited, whose enterprising spirit gave us hopes of success which were afterwards confirmed by the services of the corps.

It was to be regretted that the Lusitanian youths, who crowded from all directions to the standards of this Legion, exceeded by far the means of their immediate clothing and equipment; but the zeal and exertions of the British, together with the concurrence and assistance of the Portuguese officers, and the willingness and obedience of the soldiers, in a short time enabled the British officers to effect the complete organization of three battalions of light infantry, some cavalry, and a brigade of artillery, with four six-pounders and two howitzers; the entire consisting of about two thousand effective men, well disciplined, clothed and appointed; the uniform of the infantry was green, that of the cavalry green with white facings, and the artillery the same with black facings.

The urgent necessity which appeared to Sir Robert of immediately taking the field with this small division, for the purpose of co-operating in the defence of Portugal, (active operations being about to commence,) prevented him from waiting for an additional supply of clothing and appointments for the remainder of the Legion then at Oporto, the complete establishment of which would otherwise have taken place at this time.

The 1st division of the Lusitanian Legion marched from Oporto on the 14th of December, 1808, in the direction of the eastern frontier, leaving the 2nd division of the Legion in that city, under Baron Eben, until the clothing and appointments should arrive from England for their equipment, and giving the baron positive orders, when that should be accomplished, immediately to proceed to unite that division with the 1st for its support, as a corps of reserve; however, these orders, and necessary instructions, most extraordinary to relate, were not complied with, and the consequences resulting therefrom were the cause of no small derangement of the plans and operations which Sir Robert Wilson intended pursuing.

It may not be considered amiss here to give a short sketch of the affairs at this period in the Peninsula.

The British force, which had disembarked in August under Sir Arthur Wellesley,[4] engaged and defeated the French Army under General Junot, with considerable loss, at Roleia and Vimeira, and was in pursuit of the enemy who had fled towards Lisbon, when Sir Harry Burrard, his senior officer, landed and joined the army, and suspended the pursuit of the vanquished enemy; afterwards Sir Hugh Dalrymple arrived, and another British force of ten thousand men under Sir John Moore, with a brigade of hussars under Lord Paget; therefore the situation of the conquered enemy, shut up in the vicinity of Lisbon, with the sea and Tagus on one side, and a British army, nearly double the number of that which had before routed them, and had four times the number of cavalry, on the other side, may be easily conceived.

However, what the bravery and discipline of the French officers and soldiers were inadequate to effect against British troops of inferior numbers in the field, their general acquired in the cabinet; as most unaccountable to relate, a convention [5] was made at Cintra, signed by the British generals, with Sir Hugh Dalrymple at their head, acquiescing in the proposed terms of the vanquished and forlorn enemy, that they should be embarked on board British vessels, and conveyed home with their arms and ammunition, artillery, horses, and baggage, &c. &c.; the greater part of the latter being the plunder, church plate, &c. taken from the Portuguese inhabitants and converted into money.

Thus, instead of the discretional surrender of the enemy, so naturally to be expected, they were sent to France, from whence they marched direct into Spain, to unite with their armies there, and again oppose the British force; their embarkation was a melancholy scene to the unfortunate inhabitants, and fired with indignation the victorious heroes of Roleia and Vimeira.

This British Army afterwards marched under Sir John Moore, to co-operate with the Spanish armies opposed to the enemy in the north of Spain, where it formed a junction with another British force under Sir David Baird, who had disembarked at Corunna; the unfortunate result of which, in consequence of the hopes entertained of the effective strength and co-operation of the Spaniards, is unnecessary to mention. The Loyal Lusitanian Legion proved at this time their steadiness and discipline, so justly recorded, but previous to their march from Oporto, it is necessary to state that on the French troops, which garrisoned the fortress of Almeida, being convoyed by a detachment

---

4. *Vide* Appendix, B.
5. *Vide* Appendix, C.

of the 6th British regiment of foot to that town for embarkation, in conformity to the convention of Cintra, the inhabitants of that city, together with the neighbouring peasantry, rose and crowded to the harbour to prevent the embarkation of their property which was thus in possession of the French; and they were so enraged against those plunderers that they would have put them all to death had they been permitted.

However just their indignation might be considered on this occasion, Sir Robert Wilson, who commanded at Oporto, naturally conceived it to be his duty to comply with the convention of Cintra and insist on the embarkation of the enemy, &c. according to the terms therein specified.

It was here the subordination and soldier-like conduct of the Loyal Lusitanian Legion was first evinced, by supporting the British detachment in obedience to orders against the armed mob, which amounted to some thousands, and who had even brought cannon to the beach for the purpose of effecting their object; the predicament in which these young troops were placed was most critical, opposing so many thousands of the populace, and supporting the French against their countrymen, but the embarkation was at length effected with a good deal of difficulty, without any very serious consequences, but that of the baggage did not succeed so well.

Much credit is due to Sir Robert Wilson and his officers for their exertions on this occasion; they were supported by a corps of Spaniards, under the command of the Marquis of Valladaris, who happened to arrive at Oporto about this period, and assisted equally in quelling these disturbances and restoring tranquillity to the inhabitants.

Sir Robert Wilson and the British officers[6] attached to the Legion marched with the 1st division from Oporto on the 14th December, 1808, (with the exception of Baron Eben, left at Oporto with the 2nd division, who was to follow as soon as possible,) taking the direction of Almeida and Ciudad Rodrigo, through which places the British Army, under Sir John Moore, had passed a short time before. The line of march was through Penifiel and Amaranths, along the right bank of the River Douro, through Mezon Frio to Passa de Regoa, where

---

6. These British officers were Colonels Mayne, Baron Eben, Baron Perponger, Lieut.-Colonel Grant, Captain Charles, Aide de Camp to Sir Robert, Captain Lillie, who had been with the British army under Sir Arthur Wellesley, and volunteered to remain with the Legion, and Captains Ruman and Western, Drs. Millengen and Bolman.

we crossed the Douro and proceeded to Lamago;[7] the reception we met with from the Portuguese during our march was truly hospitable, having brought us in the kindest manner to their houses; and the gratitude and attention evinced particularly to the British officers for the interest they seemed to take in their cause, was to them particularly flattering.

The weather had hitherto been very fine; however, on our march from Lamago, the rain poured on us in torrents, continuing for several days without intermission; but, as it was conceived the affairs at that period would not permit us to delay our inarch, we were obliged to proceed, notwithstanding the floods. The roads we passed, were deemed nearly impracticable; and to many who may be unacquainted Math the state of them in this country at certain periods of the year, it may appear extraordinary to state that we were actually obliged to swim our horses; and it was with the greatest exertion and difficulty we were enabled to bring forward our artillery, being obliged to take the beasts from the guns, and officers and men, hand in hand, pulled them through the waters, which in many places reached up to their shoulders; and as an example to junior ranks we remarked our leaders among the number.

We at length arrived with considerable difficulty and inconvenience at Pinhel,[8] a bishop's see, three leagues west of Almeida, and four of the Spanish frontier; here the corps halted for a few days to make the necessary arrangements for the commencement of active operations, as well as to *descansar,* (rest), after their severe and fatiguing march from Oporto, which they bore with great patience and fortitude, and only seemed anxious to come in contact with the enemies of their country, manifesting much confidence in their officers, and giving us reason to anticipate the subsequent good conduct they displayed when opportunities offered.

However, an unfavourable change took place at this period in the cause of the Peninsula, which cast a universal damp on the Spaniards and Portuguese, by the retrograde movement of the main British force under Sir John Moore,[9] on the success of which the patriots of the Peninsula had cast their eyes as the means of their salvation from the

7. Lamago is an Episcopal city and stands on the Douro, surrounded by mountains: it was anciently peopled by Laconians, and restored by Trajan, who gave it the name of Urbs Lamacoenorum.
8. The Corregidoria of Pinhel forms fifty-five towns: the city is nothing remarkable, and is fortified in the old way.
9. *Vide* Appendix, D.

French yoke.

This British Army having been pursued by a far superior force of the enemy, the British general deemed it unadvisable to risk a battle, and turned his mind to the security and the re-embarkation of his troops, being unsupported by any allied corps; in consequence of which the few British troops and stores that had been then on their way to join the British Army were immediately countermanded; some to Oporto and others to Lisbon, for which places they proceeded with all possible dispatch; the general idea then entertained, from the immense forces of the enemy, together with the movement of the British troops towards the coasts, was, that too sanguine a hope had been entertained of the state of the Spanish armies, and that no zealous co-operation could be expected from their generals; and that the British Army, unaided and unsupported, had resolved on evacuating the country.

Under such circumstances the situation of the Loyal Lusitanian Legion may be easier conceived than expressed; orders had been received from British general officers for our retreat, and intimation had been received likewise by Sir Robert Wilson from Lieutenant General Sir John Cradock, commander of the forces in Portugal, of its having been his wish that the British officers of the Legion should withdraw and provide for their own personal safety: we therefore were rather awkwardly circumstanced, having entered the Portuguese service and embarked in their cause, and finding the country on the eve of evacuation by the British, and invaded by the French. And if the British Army had embarked at Lisbon, in all probability the retreat of the corps would have been cut off by Marshal Soult, (for Marshal Soult, on the 28th of February, with 16,000 men, did capture Oporto, and another French corps then at Placentia were expected to move down the Tagus.) Sir Robert Wilson communicated their situations to the British officers with him, leaving it at their option either to go or stay.

But they considered that as they then conceived themselves really to be in the service of Portugal, that it would be highly disgraceful at this critical juncture, and inconsistent with the character of British soldier and with the principles by which their conduct had hitherto been guided, to leave this service; they all consequently determined on not abandoning their brethren in arms, but to remain and share the fate of the Portuguese officers and men whose confidence they had gained, and whom they had brought to the frontiers for the purpose of defending their country, well armed and perfectly equipped for active and immediate service.

On the evacuation of the garrison of Almeida [10] by the British troops, under Brigadier General Cameron, consisting of the 45th and 97th regiments, retiring to Lisbon, Colonel Mayne was by that officer appointed his successor,[11] to secure the removal of the valuable British stores deposited in this fortress, for the expected campaigns of Sir John Moore's army. The garrison consisted of the Portuguese troops of the line already there, and a detachment of the Loyal Lusitanian Legion.

Sir Robert immediately marched into Spain, moving in the direction of Ciudad Rodrigo [12] his advance, consisting of two companies of infantry, a squadron of cavalry, and two guns, commanded by Captain Lillie. Sir Robert having pushed across the Spanish frontier, resolved on placing his corps in front of the garrisons of Almeida and Ciudad Rodrigo, in the direction of Salamanca,[13] where he occupied a very extensive line of country with the Loyal Lusitanian Legion, which was reinforced afterwards by some Spanish troops and Portuguese cavalry, (the line of country thus occupied, extending from Almeida on the left flank to the almost inaccessible Sierra de Francia which protected the right flank, with Ciudad Rodrigo in the rear, garrisoned by six thousand Spaniards,) and exactly in the way of a French corps, moving at that period towards the south, to join Marshal Victor, whose advance this movement had the desired effect of checking; for the French, not being aware of the number or description of the troops

10. Almeida is a strong fortification; six royal bastions of stone, and as many ravelins; a good ditch and a covered way. On a lofty mound, in the centre of the town, is a citadel remarkable for strength, with magazines bomb proof; within the walls are wells of water, and near it is a fine spring.

11. *Vide* Appendix, E.

12. Ciudad Rodrigo stands on a stone rock on the banks of the Agueda; a large square tower with battlements and loop holes overlooks the bridge, and you enter the fortress with an idea it is a strong place, but it is an irregular fortification, and far otherwise. The streets in the town are very bad and narrow, and there is nothing remarkable but a cathedral which is of tolerable beauty.

13. Salamanca famous among the Romans, and familiar to the readers of Gil Blas, is chiefly placed on three sand-stone hills in an inlet of the Tonnes, a few leagues before it falls into the, Douro. The vicinity of Salamanca, by the river, is divided into cornfields, and in the neighbourhood are the estates of the Duke of Alva. There is here a handsome Roman bridge over the Tormes, in the centre of which is a square tower, and a gateway which formerly contained a portcullis; this object and the towers and domes of the buildings of the city form an imposing spectacle. The city is entered from the bridge by a triumphal arch of the Romans, from which the principal street descends. The university of Salamanca long attracted students from every part of Europe; but is now no longer celebrated.

they had to contend with, very quietly and very fortunately for us desisted from any attempt to move forward.

The cause of this event may appear more probable when it is understood that every precaution had been taken to conceal our real strength from the enemy; and our allies likewise conceived our force to be considerably greater than it really was. This able disposition, made by the leaders of the allied troops, had the good effect of inspiring the patriots in the neighbourhood with fresh confidence; and it tended most considerably to dissipate that gloom which had spread over the country in consequence of the late unfortunate change in the campaign; at the same time it afforded the Spaniards an opportunity and time to add to the defensive state of the neighbouring garrisons, by altering and strengthening many points which contributed a good deal to the subsequent resistance made by them when invested.

In proportion as the movements revived the spirits of our allies, so did they likewise strike a panic into our advancing enemy, who, we afterwards understood, expected to meet with no opposition until they got to Lisbon, where they heard the British had retired to, and were preparing for embarkation, having dismantled the batteries and destroyed the works in the neighbourhood; however, they were not a little surprised to find a large tract of country occupied in their front, by troops dressed in British uniform and commanded by British officers, the strength of which they were unable to ascertain; they likewise understood that the fortresses of Ciudad Rodrigo and Almeida were well-garrisoned and in a good state of defence.

The French general was consequently induced to halt, not conceiving his means adequate to undertake the sieges of two such fortresses in an effective state of defence, with a disposable force under British generals, the strength of which he was ignorant of, or to oppose a corps, by which his advance posts had been attacked on several occasions, and some piquets surprised and captured; he therefore took up a position in the neighbourhood of Salamanca, leaving his advanced posts a few leagues in front of that city which had made no opposition to his entrance. We even understood afterwards that the enemy expected to be attacked, and we found by intercepted dispatches that they reported Brigadier General Wilson's corps to be ten or twelve thousand men, supported by the garrisons of Almeida and Ciudad Rodrigo, containing as many more troops.

In consequence of these circumstances the Supreme Junta of Spain conferred the command of the entire of the Spanish troops, in the kingdom of Leon, on Sir Robert Wilson, which enabled him, aided by the British officers, to concert his arrangements on a larger scale.

The British troops, that had remained in Portugal, were by this time assembled at Lisbon, preparing for embarkation and evacuating the country; they had caused the batteries even of Lisbon to be dismantled, having given up the intention of its defence, under the general idea that prevailed concerning the state of affairs at that period. But on their being apprised of the unexpected stop that had been put to the rapid advance of the enemy, the embarkation of the troops and stores was withheld, and our affairs not seeming to bear such a forlorn aspect (as was a little before conceived) from Sir Robert Wilson's and Colonel Mayne's dispatches to Sir John Cradock, a much more favourable and more satisfactory line of conduct was determined on: for though it appeared that the enemy had obliged the main British Army to embark with considerable loss, yet this they now imagined was not the only regular army to oppose them, and they gave up the idea that the subsequent conquest of the Peninsula was a matter of course; although they had obtained possession of the capital of Madrid, and established the French Government there after defeating all who opposed them.

Buonaparte, who had himself been at Madrid with a large portion of his army, had withdrawn, leaving his brother Joseph on the Spanish throne, and was directing his operations against other continental powers, then making an effort to obtain their own independence in co-operating with the Peninsula in the common cause of Europe against the powerful arm of France, striking the last blow for the subjugation of the continent. But King Joseph Buonaparte found that the French force left in Spain did not succeed *as he expec*ted, in overrunning the country, and reported to the emperor the unexpected circumstance of the inadequacy of his means for deciding the conquest of the Peninsula.

The salvation of Portugal was, at this critical period, in a great measure owing to the enterprising and distinguished services of the Loyal Lusitanian Legion under the British officers; for if the evacuation of the country by the British troops had taken place, a French army of eight or ten thousand men could have marched direct to Lisbon, where there could not be collected a regular effective force at that time, of half that number to oppose them.

The Legion continued to occupy the same tract of country already stated, affording continual annoyances to the enemy, who had been scattered over the towns in the vicinity of Salamanca, for the purpose of plundering the inhabitants; and Colonel D'Urban, now Brigadier General in the Portuguese service, and many enterprising British officers,[14] had been attracted towards this corps, by its already acquired fame, and attached themselves to its fortunes.

In one enterprise, Sir Robert, accompanied by the British officers and some Legion dragoons, galloped into the French outpost at the village of Labobada, suddenly surprised them in their houses, making them all prisoners, after a short resistance, in which they were overpowered. Captain Picaluci of the Lusitanian light horse, acting *aide-de-camp* to Colonel Mayne, was the only officer killed on this occasion, who having received a carbine ball through the heart, instantly expired, while leading on his men in a most gallant manner. The prisoners being disarmed, were sent into the woods under an escort of Spanish peasants, to whom we had given their arms.

A considerable body of the enemy's cavalry having obtained information of this successful enterprise, advanced; and being far superior to us in numbers, obliged us to retire contented with the capture we had made. But in skirmishing with them, Lieutenant L'Estrange of the 71st Regiment was taken prisoner, mounted on one of the French horses that had been taken, and which he unfortunately conceived better than his own. General D'Urban and Lieutenant-Colonel Grant particularly distinguished themselves on this occasion.

And again, we received intimation of the enemy's having made a requisition for money and horses, at the town of Ledesma, on the River Tormes, which was to have been ready on a certain day, to a considerable amount, under the severe penalties of the destruction of the place, and execution of the magistrates: we resolved, therefore, on preventing such an important supply from falling into the enemy's hands, if possible; and proceeded with a squadron of cavalry, and about one hundred select infantry,[15] whom we mounted on all sorts of mules and horses that could be procured, with the intention of suddenly falling on the enemy's escort, should it appear that our force nearly equalled theirs, or that circumstances afforded us any prospect of success, in attempting thus to preserve the property of our allies.

We happened to arrive at Ledesma, quite unexpectedly; and there

---

14. Lieutenant-Colonel Wilson, and Major L'Estrange, later Lieutenant Colonel of the 31st regiment.

15. The Legion had been joined by a good many British soldiers, cavalry and infantry, stragglers, sick, and prisoners, who escaped from Sir John Moore's army.

found the *junta* in state ready for the reception of their rapacious and dreaded enemy, for the purpose of delivering up to them the treasure and cattle demanded. We immediately concluded, that the most effectual way of preventing the above booty from falling into the hands of the enemy, would be to have it removed out of their reach, by sending it to the *junta* of Ciudad Rodrigo; it was consequently resigned to us, and we delivered it over to the *junta* of Ciudad Rodrigo. We afterwards understood that we were scarce an hour gone, when the enemy entered in considerable force from Salamanca, and were most disagreeably surprised at their unexpected disappointment, not finding either the horses or money, which they had understood were ready for their acceptance, and were consequently most vehemently enraged.

They would probably have wreaked their vengeance on the unfortunate and innocent inhabitants, had not the *junta* shewn Sir Robert Wilson's receipt, specifying the number of horses and quantity of money He had received;—and for their own justification, they stated his demand having been seconded by a military force, in consequence of which they were induced to comply, being unable to act otherwise. This had the desired effect of saving them and the inhabitants from destruction; but to prevent any thing of the kind for the future, the French sent a garrison there, which was shortly afterwards alarmed by a detachment of the Legion under the command of Lieutenant Colonel Grant, who attacked their advance posts by night, and surprised them sitting round their fires in the woods, by falling on them suddenly, and killed or dispersed the whole; those who escaped fled into the town, and the enemy were induced to confine their garrison afterwards within the walls of the place.

Scarcely a day passed without some enterprise of this nature occurring, which tended most considerably to the annoyance of the enemy, never permitting them a moment's tranquillity, and it likewise did not suffer them to scatter small plundering parties over the country, never knowing when and where they might expect to be attacked. On this service we derived considerable advantage from the assistance of the Spanish guerrillas, and from the attachment and fidelity manifested by the native peasantry, who bore an inveterate enmity towards the French on all occasions, and who cordially assisted in constantly obtaining us the most correct information of all the enemy's movements and strength.

The conduct of the Loyal Lusitanians, and the enterprising operations and able dispositions made by their officers, rendered these important services not only to Portugal and Spain, but to all Europe, in the common cause of its independence, arresting the progress of the enemy advancing into Portugal (at that period deemed inadequate to any resistance), and gaining time for the British government, on being acquainted with the real state of affairs, to send another expedition to Portugal under Lord Wellington, who on his arrival in the Peninsula was enabled to defeat Marshal Soult in the North, at Oporto, while the corps under General Lapisse [16] was prevented by the Legion from entering Portugal by Almeida, to co-operate with Marshal Soult.

The native valour and steadiness of the Portuguese troops, with their willingness and obedience to British discipline, and confidence and attachment to British officers, so strongly manifested on these occasions, induced the British government to pursue the original intention of extending the system (which had been so fortunately justified by the distinguished services of the Loyal Lusitanian Legion) to the whole Portuguese Army, and General Beresford was sent to Lisbon in March, 1809, with British officers, arms, appointments, &c. for the organisation of the whole army.

The Legion still continued to annoy the enemy, from whom constant desertions took place, in consequence of our having had hand-bills circulated amongst them, written in different languages, which induced many, principally those who had been serving by force in the French Army, to fly to us for protection, having been given their choice to be sent to their native country, or enter the British service. We now had two battalions of the corps at Puerto de Bainos, an important pass, to intercept the communications between Lapisse at Salamanca, and the French Army under Marshal Victor, opposed to a Spanish force under General Cuesta, on the Tagus, in the neighbourhood of Almaraz, which was of considerable importance, and annoyed and deranged the plans of the enemy in a very great degree.

The command of this pass was given to Colonel Mayne, who had been removed from Almeida, when it appeared there was no likelihood of the enemy's advancing, or investing that fortress, and when he had seen, under his immediate direction and superintendence, all the valuable stores to the amount of £150,000 sterling, safely conveyed from thence and secured at Lamago.

Colonel Mayne added considerably to the natural strength of this important pass of Bainos, by mining the roads through it, and having his artillery placed in the most commanding situations, lest these

16. Afterwards killed in action.

corps of the enemy should attempt to force the pass, to form a junction through it; he also at this time, in compliance with the desire of the inhabitants, assisted in fortifying the town of Bejar, the vaunted residence of the dukes of that title.[17]

A large convoy with important dispatches was intercepted about this period by our guerrillas, and those of the escort who had not been put to the sword brought in prisoners to Colonel Mayne. With the dispatches there were Paris mails for Madrid, containing many public and official communications, which were of great importance to be acquainted with, and likewise many private and affectionate love letters, and tender remembrances from the Parisian fair; the former official dispatches served for our leader's consideration, while the latter amused the leisure hours of our party, and the subject was peculiarly adapted to the lonely and romantic scenes in the lofty Sierra d'Estrella; we even found some French butter in the mail for His Majesty, King Joseph, from his imperial brother, amongst many other tokens of his royal favour and affection. The seals of King Joseph's new government were captured in this mail, and there were some trifling presents for the officers of the French Army: among these a watch for the Intendant General Danet, which has a reference to a curious concurrence.[18]

We likewise at this time intercepted a dispatch, wherein Lapisse mentioned his having marched a corps of 6000 men to reinforce Victor; but on finding Puerto de Bainos occupied by the division under Colonel Mayne, with artillery, they were obliged to return. General Lapisse was determined then to know our force, which he endeavoured to make us concentrate, by advancing towards Ciudad Rodrigo, which he failed in doing, but he made some attacks on our out-posts with success.

Major L'Estrange commanded a post at the bridge of the Ecla, which was attacked by a considerable force of the enemy, who succeeded in obliging it to retire after some resistance, in which Major L'Estrange was made prisoner. Colonel John Wilson's post was likewise attacked by General Hammerstein's regiment of *chasseurs à cheval*, in which, after a gallant contest in a close intricate country, the enemy, losing considerably by the well directed fire of the Portuguese and Spaniards, were very happy to retire.

After this the enemy advanced to Ciudad Rodrigo, with the entire

---

17. The *junta* of Bejar presented Colonel Mayne with the sword of the Dukes of Bejar, as a token of their gratitude on this occasion.
18. *Vide* Appendix, F.

of the force that was in the vicinity of Salamanca, reduced at this time to 7000 effective men, and summoned this garrison for the first time to surrender, threatening, in case of refusal, to put the garrison to the sword. Lieutenant Colonel Grant with a detachment of the Legion, with four guns, remained outside the works, and received the summons, brought by a French officer, accompanied by a trumpeter, who wanted to enter the garrison with it; this he was refused, but his summons was forwarded to the governor; and the enemy continued to advance during the temporary armistice towards the gates of the garrison; the Legion guns placed on an eminence in front of the works, immediately let them know, by opening a brisk and destructive fire on their advancing columns, that they were acting against the customs of war, which induced them, on sustaining some loss, to halt, and consequently the fire ceased.

The governor's reply to the summons was, that consistent with his duty as governor of that fortress, he could not think of acceding to it, even if he saw a greater necessity for so doing than appeared to him at present. We now expected that the place would be immediately invested; however, after a sharp contest between the Legion and the enemy, it appeared they manifested no very serious intention of undertaking a siege, and it was consequently concluded they had expected to frighten the garrison to surrender.

Shortly afterwards another summons was sent by General Lapisse, trusting the Spanish general and garrison would not allow themselves to be misled by British officers recommending their resistance to a summons *in the name of His Majesty the King of Spain*; and that if they did, the result must prove fatal to the garrison and inhabitants, as he should be reduced to the necessity of giving up the place to the common soldiery on its fall, to plunder, &c. &c.; he at the same time suggested, that if the governor opened his gates and acknowledged King Joseph, he should himself be most handsomely rewarded, and continue to hold the government of the garrison, and that the inhabitants should experience the kindest treatment from His Imperial Majesty's armies. The verbal reply sent back was that the answer to the last summons was wadded in the ordnance of the garrison, which they should receive on their farther advance. Lieutenant-Colonel Grant distinguished himself most particularly on this occasion, and in another brilliant affair with a column of the same army at San Felices, on the Agueda, which is detailed in Sir Robert Wilson's dispatch.[19]

---

19. *Vide* Appendix, G.

The French general, finding the capture of this garrison could not be effected without a regular siege, being well fortified and strongly garrisoned, and the project of frightening it to surrender having failed, concluded, that his entrance into Portugal by this road, to co-operate with Soult, was not to be effected. His communication with Salamanca in his rear, was likewise cut off by the two other battalions of the Legion, and the different other corps then under the command of Colonel Mayne; and at this very time the peasantry all rose, in the neighbourhood for many miles round, and joined us.

The enemy finding himself thus beset, on all sides, and his communication with Salamanca and his rear cut off, made a sudden movement towards the south, for the purpose of endeavouring to form a junction with Victor's corps on the left bank of the Tagus, by crossing that river at the bridge of Alcantara. By this unexpected movement of the enemy, Colonel Mayne's division was brought rather in his front, and he moved on Cacillas de Flores, making an endeavour to possess himself of the pass of Peralis, which headed the enemy's column, and through which it was necessary for him to pass to proceed to Alcantara, which, had the colonel had sufficient time to effect, would have enabled him to engage the enemy in that very strong position, and arrest his progress, until the surrounding Spanish and Portuguese bodies united for a general attack.

The colonel consequently moved on with the Legion and some cavalry, having previously sent forward Captains Lillie and Charles, for the purpose of observing the movement of the enemy's column. These officers, after crossing the extensive forests between Cacillas des Flores and Peralis, at length came in sight of the French division on the main road, which passes the village of Paio. While they were making their reconnoissance from the rising ground immediately above the village of Paio, a French column was passing close underneath in the direction of Peralis, and a plundering party of the French, with some waggons, separated from the main body for the purpose of ransacking that village, through which those officers had just passed, and whose return was intercepted by the enemy having obtained possession of it, which was done unnoticed by them, in consequence of the close wood which surrounds it.

They therefore found themselves cut off, there being no passage for horsemen, except through the village, and their only alternative was to surrender as prisoners, or make an attempt at running the risk of galloping through the village in the enemy's possession, which they immediately resolved on, and suddenly passing through the French soldiers, with which the place was thronged, got clear out, without even a shot being fired at them, or any attempt made to stop them. On their getting into the wood at the other side, they came suddenly on a few Spanish dragoons, who, taking them for French cavalry riding towards them, knowing a considerable number to have been in the place they came from, galloped off to Colonel Mayne, whom they met within two leagues of the place, advancing towards it, and acquainted him of their adventure.

Colonel Mayne ascertained from these officers, the particulars of the enemy's movements, and finding he was unable to secure the pass of Peralis, the enemy being then in possession of it, he endeavoured, if possible, to cut off the detachment at Paio; he therefore moved forward with his cavalry as quick as possible, but found they had fled on his approach, however, he pursued them closely, and made some prisoners, but was unable to retake their plunder, which they had sent a considerable distance in advance.

Sir Robert Wilson, who had been also pursuing the enemy from Ciudad Rodrigo with a few dragoons, came to Paio at night, having made a considerable number of prisoners that day and the day before. Colonels Wilson and Grant likewise united at Paio, from whence we all proceeded next day, and continued the pursuit of the enemy, uniting all the different bodies for that purpose. Our force at this time amounted to many thousands. We pursued the enemy with our whole force for two days, making a number of prisoners in the different skirmishes with his rear. The pursuit was continued with great success, and harassed the enemy excessively, who supposed they were followed by a very large army.

On their arrival at Alcantara,[20] an ancient and renowned city, which is fortified, and the chief resort of the knights of that name, and which is situated on the left bank of the River Tagus in Spain, and close to the Portuguese frontier, the inhabitants endeavoured, as much as possible, to obstruct the passage of the river, over which there is a most magnificent and ancient bridge of Roman architecture, built by Trajan, at the extremities of the battlements of which they had constructed a kind of abbatis across the road, which had been excavated to the depth of eighteen or twenty feet; the enemy finding himself so pressed in his rear, resolved on attempting it by storm, consequently those obstacles, however strong, were of little avail, being unprotected

20. This town was taken by Lord Galway in 1706.

by a regular garrison, or, in fact, any military force.

The bridge having been passed, after the town had been cannonaded for some time, and the gates forced open, the revenge and cruelty of the enemy were exercised in the most barbarous manner on the unfortunate and helpless inhabitants who had been found in the town, or taken in endeavouring to effect their escape. They were butchered in the most brutal manner in every direction, and it may be doubted whether the annals of history describe so inhuman a spectacle as that unfortunate place presented on its evacuation by its treacherous and cruel enemy, who performed acts of cruelty and barbarity there that would disgrace the most savage and uncivilised of mankind.

Two squadrons of our advanced cavalry, one Spanish, under Don Carlos D'Espagne, and the other Portuguese, under Captain Lillie, of the Legion, arrived in the night in front of Alcantara, immediately after the French had entered it in the evening, and continued near the town, under the command of Lieutenant-Colonel Grant. At daybreak the following morning, they moved down towards the bridge, and obtained intimation that the enemy had marched out on the Caceres road. The scene witnessed by the above officers on entering the town, exceeds all description; the houses in many parts of this unfortunate place were in flames, and the passage of the streets actually obstructed by mangled bodies of all descriptions lying in heaps; in other places, piles of furniture, and many valuable articles that could not be brought away had been erected in front of the houses of some of the principal inhabitants, and had been set fire to, and the mutilated bodies of the unfortunate owners covered with wounds, were thrown on the piles, and there found burning in a most shocking manner.

They were afterwards recognised, with a good deal of difficulty, by some of their unfortunate families, on their return from the woods and mountains to which they had fled, and the melancholy sadness and sorrow depicted in the countenances of these unhappy people, recognizing the mangled bodies of their nearest friends and relations, lying in heaps about the streets, is not to be described. Mixed with human bodies were likewise those of dogs and pigs; in fact, every animal of whatever description the invaders had met with, fell a victim to the unexampled cruelty of those horrid and despicable ruffians. Even the chapels, and places of divine worship, did not escape their ravages; they broke open the doors, and polluted the altars of those sacred edifices, carrying off all the plate and valuables they could find.

Not permitting even the deceased to rest in peace and quietness;

they raised the tombstones which form the floors of the cathedrals and other places of worship in these countries, and broke open the coffins, in hopes of being able to discover some hidden treasure that might have hitherto escaped their search. Even the beautiful paintings and scripture pieces which ornament so considerably those magnificent buildings, were mangled and destroyed, and the figures of our Saviour and the Saints, beautifully carved, as large as life, were knocked about, and mutilated in a most depraved manner. Our cavalry, with a great deal of difficulty, effected their passage through the streets, and found that the enemy had continued their march, with considerable dispatch, in the direction of Brozas, taking with them their sacrilegious plunder.

The enemy had destroyed the provisions of alt sorts that they could not themselves consume, and our cavalry were obliged to move immediately into Portugal, about eight miles distant, having been a considerable time without subsistence of any description either for themselves or their horses, leaving the unfortunate city of Alcantara to experience for the first time in these campaigns, the misery and shocking devastations of uncivilized war.

Major-General Beresford was at Thomar a this period, organizing the Portuguese Army, and had ordered the Legion into Portugal, and Sir Robert himself to Thomar, for the purpose of giving him a different command with the force then about to proceed towards the north of Portugal, for the purpose of expelling the French corps, under Marshal Soult, which had remained unmolested in that quarter, and was then at Oporto, to which place, as was observed before, he advanced, unsupported by any other cooperating body. After General Lapisse's attempt on the eastern frontier had been so fortunately frustrated by the Legion, Soult was attacked by the allies under Sir Arthur Wellesley, in May, and routed with considerable loss, including his artillery and baggage. The fugitives took the direction of Gallicia, from which they had entered, and were closely pursued into that province.

The Loyal Lusitanian Legion was at this time attached to the corps of the allied army under Major-General Mackenzie, which had been formed on the right bank of the Tagus, as a corps of observation on the enemy's force, who had been opposed to the Spanish general Cuesta, in Spanish Estremadura, of which corps the Loyal Lusitanian Legion formed the advance at Alcantara, under Colonel Mayne, where it had an opportunity of particularly distinguishing itself and the commander, in a most brilliant action, which gained it the admiration of the whole Peninsula; the particulars of which shall be hereafter related.

It must appear extraordinary, that nothing has been mentioned of our second division, which had never joined us, under Baron Eben, but which junction it was so natural to expect would have been effected long ere this, in obedience to the orders he had received; and it may easily be concluded what an acquisition such an organised, well clothed and appointed reinforcement, would have been to the corps, during the late arduous undertakings to which it had been exposed; and in proportion as it would have so considerably increased our means of acting, so it would, in like manner, have added additional lustre to the result of our undertakings.

But the noble baron, on some account or other, deferred his march from Oporto until Marshal Soult had effected his entrance through Chaves, into Portugal, when the baron (who had not participated in the honours and well-acquired fame which had so eminently distinguished the Legion from its late exertions) set out from Oporto with the second division, 1200 strong, not for the purpose of joining his corps, according to the arrangement already made, but of attacking Marshal Soult, a renowned Marshal of France, at the head of 10,000 veteran troops.

Most certainly the defeat of such a corps by Baron Eben, at the head of 1,200 inexperienced Portuguese troops, would have been unparalleled, consequently the fame and glory of such an inconceivable success would have been productive of the most brilliant honours and rewards, and would certainly have covered any remarks that might have hitherto been made as to his delay at Oporto: it would at the same time have far exceeded whatever the comparatively small services of the first division had achieved, under every exertion and toil, and would have completely overbalanced the fame they had so justly acquired.

The Portuguese general, Bernardino Frere, who was commander-in-chief of the army, being about this time accused of treason by a lawless mob, was, without farther inquiry, waylaid by them, and himself and his staff murdered; the command of the army was conferred on Baron Eben, but not by Marshal Beresford, by whom he was superseded as soon as possible. The baron, however, continued his march against Marshal Soult, but the result was not so favourable as we could wish, for the baron's return to Oporto was much quicker than his advance; and it was with much regret we found that our second division, after being dispersed, continued to fly in all directions, in the utmost disorder, and the greater part were disarmed by the peasantry; who, finding them scattered about by twos and threes, without any officers, and quitting that part of the country into which the enemy were advancing, concluded that such fine arms and appointments, &c. which had but just arrived from England, might be meant for a better use, and laid hold of them for the purpose of protecting themselves and their families from the small plundering parties of the enemy.

This, alas! was the fate of the second division of the Legion, which Sir Robert Wilson had entrusted to the baron, relying on him for the junction of it with the first, as soon as possible.

As we found this unfortunate and scattered division directed their course to Lisbon, Captain Lillie was detached from the first division to that city, for the purpose of reassembling them, and marching them to join Colonel Mayne when completed with arms, appointments, &c. which, after a little time, was effected, and when they joined the first division, they amounted to 800 rank and file, and Baron Eben remained at Lisbon during the succeeding campaigns.

While the allies under Sir Arthur Wellesley were in pursuit of Soult's corps in the north of Portugal, in May, 1809, Victor, not knowing of our successes in that quarter, moved with a corps of 12,000 men, commanded by himself in person, from Spanish Estremadura towards Portugal, for the purpose of making a diversion in Soult's favour, and on his arriving at the bridge of Alcantara, which was occupied by the Loyal Lusitanian Legion, which formed the advance of General Mackenzie's corps, under the command of Colonel Mayne, he found he must force his way over it.

Colonel Mayne had made the necessary dispositions for the defence of the bridge and the position he had taken.

Lieutenant Colonel Grant, who was in advance, retired before the enemy's corps, after some skirmishing on the 12th of May, on which day the enemy entered Alcantara, which on account of its being on the left bank of the Tagus it was necessary to evacuate, for the purpose of defending the passage of the river, which was the only object, consequently this unfortunate city was again exposed to the ravages of its wanton enemies. The position taken up by Colonel Mayne was on an eminence, the opposite side of the river from Alcantara, where some batteries had been erected. There was a battalion of militia also under Colonel Mayne's command, which including all did not exceed two thousand men. However our means might be inadequate to ultimate success, still it was a great object at that period to retard as much as possible the entrance of the enemy into Portugal in that direction, as it would bring him in rear of the allies in the north; consequently Colonel Mayne was determined to dispute the passage of the river as much as possible, in conformity to the orders he had received.

The enemy's columns having come within range of our batteries, our guns commenced a fire on them with a good deal of effect, and many shells were pitched directly into the centre of their columns, which did considerable execution. The parapets and walls of the town were soon lined by the infantry of the enemy, while they constructed batteries, which afterwards bore with a good deal of effect on our position, and particularly two which were brought to bear on our flanks. In the mean time a heavy and destructive fire of musketry had commenced on both sides.

But the enemy having brought all their artillery to bear on us, together with the concentrated fire of eleven thousand muskets, with which the houses, &c. on the opposite side were lined, we were obliged to give way; but much to the credit of the brave soldiers engaged, be it recorded, that they sustained that tremendous fire for the space of nine hours, during which the enemy could not succeed in any attempt made at carrying the bridge by storm, having suffered most considerably from the well directed fire of our sharpshooters, covered by the rocks, &c. within forty or fifty yards of the bridge, and from that to one and two hundred yards along the ascent of the heights.

However night coming on, which would evidently favour them, and especially in any attempt at carrying the bridge by storm, in which from the vast superiority of their numbers they must ultimately succeed, together with our having our small force already reduced by the loss of seven officers, and two hundred and fifty men killed and wounded, Colonel Mayne was induced, to prevent the complete sacrifice of these brave fellows under his command, to retire to the bridge of Seguro, only two leagues distant, leaving a rear guard with the cavalry, under Lieutenant Colonel Grant, to cover this movement, which was effected with the greatest steadiness and regularity, and proved these young troops to be worthy of the ancient military character of the Portuguese nation, having evinced that fortitude and gallantry at so early a period of the campaigns, which was afterwards so fully maintained, that they were reported to the British Government by Lord Wellington as "worthy of contending in the same ranks with veterans, to which they were not inferior in point of valour and discipline."

The Loyal Lusitanian Legion took up another position at the bridge of Seguro, in case the enemy should be determined on any other attempt of forcing their way into Portugal. The advance of the enemy moved towards this position, which they reconnoitred, sustaining at the same time some loss from our skirmishers in front, but finding their advance was still determined to be resisted, and possibly having obtained some intelligence of Soult's defeat, they returned without demonstrating any inclination to attack us again; and Victor marched off in the direction from whence he had advanced into Spanish Estremadura, declaring in a letter which was afterwards intercepted, that in the course of his service he never witnessed more intrepidity than was evinced by these young Portuguese soldiers at the battle of Alcantara.

The commander-in-chief's orders are annexed in the Appendix, and the gallant conduct of the Loyal Lusitanian Legion in this affair is mentioned in a manner most flattering to the officers and soldiers of that corps; noticing to the whole army in General Orders, "that although troops may be sometimes obliged to retire, at the same time they may cover themselves with glory, and merit the greatest praise."[21]

The British and Portuguese forces which had been in pursuit of Soult, returned about the end of May and beginning of June, and the British Army daily increasing, Sir Arthur Wellesley determined on moving into Spain. Sir Robert Wilson had at this time returned to his legion, and had succeeded in effecting an arrangement with Sir Arthur, that the Loyal Lusitanian Legion was to be attached to the British Army about to commence active operations in Spain, the advance of which it had the honour of forming under Sir Robert Wilson, who had likewise the 5th Portuguese Caçadores or light infantry attached to his corps, during its subsequent services in Spain, which were the only Portuguese troops at that time deemed advisable to bring on that service.

The necessary arrangements having been made, the British army was put in motion in the month of July, 1809, and proceeded into Spain by Castello Branco[21], Salvaterra, and Zarza Mayor, the Loyal Lusitanians leading in advance. We passed through Coria and Placentia[22], after which a junction was formed with the Spanish army of Gen-

21. *Vide* Appendix, I. 21. This town is placed on a granite hill, between the Liria and the Ponçul, encircled by its double wall and four gates, its flank of seven towers, and once formidable castle. There is a very fine bishop's palace, with the finest gardens and plantations in Portugal. 22. Placentia is situated in a plain surrounded by mountains, forty leagues west of Madrid. It has a castle and a few bad fortifications, and is the seat of a diocese.

eral Cuesta, which had crossed the Tagus for that purpose at Almaraz and Archibispo; and in consequence of the enemy's being in force in our front, occupying Talavera[23] de la Reyna and its neighbourhood, a general engagement was immediately expected. But on the advance of the British the enemy withdrew their troops from that place, from which circumstance it appeared that the 1st corps of the French army, which had been posted in Talavera and its vicinity, declined coming to action with the allies, until a junction had been formed of the different corps of the enemy then assembling, under King Joseph.

Our Portuguese corps under Sir Robert Wilson, had been by this time reinforced by the Spanish regiments of Seville and Merida, and we separated from the allied army, making a rapid advance along the right bank of the Alberche River in the direction of Madrid, which manoeuvre brought us round the right flank of the enemy's corps which had taken post at Talavera, In the meantime the allies continued to advance on that town, while the enemy moved across the Alberche, where it was expected a general engagement would take place, which promised a most successful result to the British arms. However the enemy finding his rear threatened by our corps, which had by this time got round his right flank, foresaw the imminent danger he was in of being cut off, should he come to an engagement with the allies on that day, consequently he abandoned his camp on the night of the 23rd, and fled in the direction of Toledo.[24]

The French official detail of those transactions states this circumstance thus:

. . . . that the combined force was on its march towards Talav-

---

23. Talavera del Reyna, on the Tagus, in New Castile, was a very populous and prosperous town, and famous for its great silk manufactures. Here are the remains of a very fine Roman temple, but nothing else of any note.

24. Toledo has always been regarded as a town of great consideration by the Romans, the Arabs, the Goths, and the Spaniards, under Charles the Fifth. It is entered from a bridge of more height than strength. It is dignified by the title of Imperial by Alphonso the Sixth, and is pre-eminent to Burgos in the Cortes. This city is famous for the temper of sword blades. The architecture of the town-house by Dominico Greco, is of great taste; and its towers, Doric and Ionic columns, and other ornaments, are well worthy of attention.

The following inscription is on the staircase in Spanish:—"Noble and judicious men who govern Toledo, leave your passions on this staircase, love, fear, and the desire of gain. For the public benefit forget private interest. Serve God who made you the pillars of this august place. Be firm and upright."

The cathedral is one of the most venerable and interesting structures in Europe.

era; while a corps of eight or ten thousand men, commanded by General Wilson, was advancing towards Escalona, along the right bank of the Alberche. The danger was imminent, and it was necessary to take decided measures.

It therefore appeared that we again succeeded in concealing our real strength from the enemy, (as the entire effective strength of our corps did not really exceed half that number,) which had the effect of being one of the principal reasons, for causing the precipitate flight of a whole French Army, under the command of Marshal the Duke of Belluno; who in the same French account gets a good deal of credit for so doing, having effected his escape from being cut off by "General Wilson's corps, which endeavoured to get in his rear."

After this it was not conceived the enemy's intention was to make a stand before the allied armies, in consequence of which we pushed on through Naval Carneiro for Madrid,[25] which had been evacuated by King Joseph and his guards taking the direction of Toledo, leaving a small garrison in the capital under General Beilliard. On our approach towards this city we were received with universal rejoicings by the natives all along the roads; and the citizens, on hearing of our approach, burst forth, manifesting the greatest demonstrations of joy and gladness at the bright prospect which opened to them of shaking off the oppressive government with which they were burthened, and of exterminating their intrusive king, with his lawless followers.

The gates of the city were thrown open to receive us, and the small French garrison overpowered, fled to the citadel, where they shut themselves up from the fury of the populace. The governor, General Beilliard, was a liberal and humane man, and notwithstanding the general tumult and uproar in the city, rode through the streets alone, entreating the inhabitants to have patience, and wait a little for the

25. Madrid, from a mean town built on a sterile spot, has become in some respects one of the finest cities in Europe. It has no suburbs, and its outline is formed by domes and spires, and in the distance the snow-topped mountains of Guardarama. A superb bridge over the Manzanares River, designed by John de Herrera, built without stones, and having a parapet breast high, upwards of seven hundred paces in length, and thirty in breadth, is a fine approach to the city, by the royal residence and the gate of Segovia: the city has also a handsome appearance when viewed from the entrance by the side of the Escurial, crossing a forest of ash trees, with agreeable pieces of water. The gate of San Vincente is new, and the palace, which is in many respects superb, is approached through it by a steep ascent. The verdure and the shade of the banks of the Manzaranes form the principal beauties of Madrid. Here is also the palace of Buen Retiro, and the so much celebrated walk of the Prado.

result of the general engagement, which he told them was about to take place at that time; and that in case the result proved successful for the allies, he should give them up the city; at the same time explaining to the people, that should the allies be unsuccessful, the inhabitants of Madrid would only expose themselves to serious consequences, resulting from the displeasure of the king, &c.

However the citizens of ail classes and descriptions flocked out to meet us for many miles, evincing every mark of loyalty and gratitude for the favourable prospect of their delivery from the French yoke, and congratulating us on the state of the capital, into which we should be received with cheer s and rejoicings, and without the least opposition from the enemy, &c. &c.

The capital was at this time unprotected; for it appeared that the enemy had formed a junction of all the troops it was in his power to unite, for the purpose of engaging the allies, and had moved them in the direction of Talavera. Madrid must therefore have surrendered to our arms: but Sir Arthur Wellesley was not aware of this circumstance, and to strengthen his own army, had countermanded Sir Robert Wilson, and thus prevented our having sufficient force to occupy Madrid; and we returned by forced marches, and arrived during the Battle of Talavera[26] in the rear of the enemy's camp, which caused him considerable alarm, and obliged him at the same time to withdraw a corps of 10,000 men to watch the movements of the Legion, and the reduction of so considerable a force from the enemy's army during the latter part of that important engagement was of no small assistance towards the great and glorious result, and the enemy commenced his retreat the following night, leaving the British heroes in possession of their well earned laurels on that memorable occasion, and the plains of Talavera strewed with many thousands of his killed and wounded.

This scene, and the town of Talavera on the day after that glorious battle, presented a most awful spectacle, and the situation of the numerous wounded and dying, the half of which could not be sufficiently attended to, was truly pitiable.

The enemy finding, after his retreat, that he was not closely pursued by the allies, halted part of his army on the 31st, but the Legion moved towards them, and obliged them to retreat; as we learn from

---

26. On the 26th, and morning of the 27th of July, the Spaniards who had advanced were retreating in the most disorderly manner. There was an affair of posts under General Mackenzie this evening, and then commenced this memorable battle. *Vide* Appendix, K.

their own dispatches,[27] which state that in consequence of intelligence of a Portuguese column having put itself in motion among the mountains to turn the right of the first corps. Marshal Victor was obliged to quit his position, and continue his retreat on Maqueda.

At this time Lord Wellington obtained information of Soult's having passed through the Puerto de Bainos, and of his arrival at Placentia in his rear, and he determined on marching to attack him, leaving General Cuesta with the Spanish Army at Talavera, who, it had been settled in a council of war, was to have remained there. At the same time this circumstance was intimated to Sir Robert Wilson, (then advanced towards Escalona.) whom Lord Wellington put in communication with General Cuesta: however, Sir Robert found that General Cuesta had unexpectedly retired from Talavera the day after Lord Wellington, and that the enemy had advanced again to it. and thereby got possession of the British hospital left there, and the unfortunate wounded, among whom were many officers of the first distinction.

In consequence of these unexpected circumstances the Loyal Lusitanian Legion endeavoured, by long marches through the mountains, to return to the British Army at Orapaza, from which we were sixty miles the day that General Cuesta evacuated Talavera, but we found that the road to Orapaza was in the enemy's possession, and that it was then too late to retire by Arzobispo. We were consequently in an alarming situation, having no retreat left unoccupied by the enemy; however, *nil desperandum,* we determined on forcing our way across the Teitar towards the mountains which separate Estremadura from Castile.

At Aldea Nueva we met a detachment of the enemy which occupied that town, which we routed from it in a short time; and understanding the enemy's corps about us had made arrangements for cutting us off, we were reduced to the necessity of making forced marches to the mountains, but we found that the town of Viranda, through which we were to pass, and at which we arrived at night, was occupied by the enemy in force, and we were under circumstances, induced to attempt carrying it by storm. We moved on quickly towards the gates, the 5th Cacadores forming the advance, but we were soon perceived by the sentries placed at the gates, and fired upon, which immediately alarmed the garrison: however we forced our way forward to the town, and found the garrison collected in the streets, who poured in a heavy volley amongst us, which was returned in an

27. *Vide* Appendix. L.

irregular manner by the Fifth Caçadores, who were in front, and who had halted, and appeared unwilling to proceed in consequence of the hot fire kept up by the enemy, the darkness of the night, and narrowness of the streets.

Sir Robert Wilson therefore ordered forward one of the battalions of the Loyal Lusitanian Legion from the rear, who eagerly advanced, proud of the circumstance, and of their selection on the occasion, and gallantly moved forward until they were brought in front, when they immediately poured in a well directed volley, and coming down instantly to the charge, advanced with cheers upon the enemy, whom they threw into greatest confusion, and drove before them at the point of the bayonet.

Having thus fortunately succeeded in effecting this important passage, we marched on without delay or interruption, the enemy having dispersed in all directions, and our loss on this occasion being inconsiderable.

We attained the Sierra Liana shortly afterwards, leaving Lieutenant-Colonel Grant with the cavalry at Viranda to follow the next day. This had the effect of deceiving the enemy, who imagined the corps still remained there, and proceeded with a new force to attack it; on which our cavalry evacuated it quietly, and ascended the pathway after the infantry towards the summit of that almost inaccessible mountain, where the enemy could not attack us on those formidable heights without sustaining the greatest loss.

Having succeeded in eluding the vigilance of these corps of the enemy, which attempted to intercept our return, and having overcome those other bodies with whom we came in contact, we proceeded to Boyoyo, through Barco d'Avila, to Bejar and Bainos, taking the direction of Portugal; but in consequence of our communication having been so long cut off from any British or allied corps, we were not aware of the changes that had taken place, or of the measures that had been adopted, or the state or situation of the different armies.

We were proceeding on the road to Grenadilha, from Puerte de Bainos, on the morning of the 12th of August, when a column of the enemy was discovered to be on the march, taking the direction of Bainos from Placentia, which happened to be Marshal Ney's corps from that part of the army that Marshal Soult commanded, and which was on its return to Salamanca, leaving Soult with the remainder at Placentia. Sir Robert Wilson consequently resolved on returning to Bainos, notwithstanding his not having artillery, (which he had received orders to leave with the British army previous to their movement from Talavera,) and he endeavoured to arrest the enemy's progress on the heights of the Puerto, leaving his advance under Lieutenant-Colonel Grant at Aldea Nueva, about a league in front of Bainos, with two companies of Spanish infantry placed in ambush, who suddenly made their appearance on the arrival of the enemy's advanced cavalry, and saluted them with a well directed volley of musketry, which did such considerable execution that they were obliged to return briskly on the main body again: however, they afterwards pushed on in considerable force, and by extending round the flanks of our advance, obliged them to retire on Bainos, which they did in a very regular manner, keeping up a brisk and destructive fire on the advancing enemy from behind the rocks, walls, &c. until they joined the main body in their rear, when the action became general.

The enemy after this brought his numerous artillery to bear on our columns, when we seriously felt the want of that powerful arm of war: however we maintained our ground for many hours (nine) notwithstanding the great superiority of their numbers. The enemy on this occasion sustained a very great loss, particularly in their *chasseurs à cheval*, when attempting to get round our flanks; but Sir Robert Wilson judging our means to be inadequate to farther resistance against such a manifest superiority of numbers, moved off his troops to his left, leaving the main road to Salamanca open for the enemy's passage.

Sir Robert Wilson had a double object in view on being induced to engage the enemy at Bainos; an evident one was, saving his corps from being attacked in the plain where they would have been exposed to a very superior force, possessing a numerous train of artillery and cavalry, the result of which must have proved fatal to it; and another was, that by engaging the enemy at the strong pass of Bainos, he might have the power of disabling a greater portion of them, and thus render the most essential service in checking their movement towards Salamanca, and consequently deranging their plans in a greater degree.

By the French account of this engagement they report their loss to be fifteen field officers and captains, with one hundred and seventy subalterns and privates killed and wounded, besides many who fell dead in the ranks from the fatigue they suffered. Their loss, however, may be justly computed at three times that number, as the French reports of their real loss seldom exceed the third part, while they generally treble that of their enemies.

They report our loss to have been on that occasion twelve hundred men left dead on the field; which, including all in killed, wounded, and missing, did not amount to four hundred, among whom there was not a field officer or captain; and many of those included in that number, reported as missing, joined us afterwards; therefore the enemy's loss may be very justly calculated to have doubled our own.

Lord Wellington's dispatches,[28] after this affair, reflect much credit on the corps. The enemy, after burying their dead, and making arrangements for removing their wounded, advanced towards Salamanca, while the Legion proceeded by Miranda del Castanas, through the pass of Peralis, towards Portugal, arriving at Castello Branco on the 24th of August, after which they joined Lord Wellington, who had at this time crossed the Tagus, and moved on Badajos and Elvas, where the British Army took up its quarters for some succeeding months, to repose and recruit their severe losses at the Battle of Talavera de la Reyna.

Marshal Beresford had collected a very large body of the Portuguese Army in the vicinity of Ciudad Rodrigo and Almeida, during those operations, and afterwards moved through the pass of Peralis, along the Portuguese frontier towards the south. And it was conceived, that, had His Excellency moved to the pass of Bainos (being well provided with artillery, &c. for its defence,) previous to Marshal Soult's movement through it in rear of the British army on Placentia, it would have tended most considerably to ensure to us those advantages, which appeared to be the probable result of the glorious victory obtained over the combined French Army at Talavera; but our hopes were for the present frustrated, by Marshal Soult's unexpected movement not being checked, and Lord Wellington then deeming it advisable to retire into Portugal with his victorious army. Had it not been for the turn this unfortunate neglect occasioned in our military prospects, Lord Wellington would have driven the French armies from the south of the Peninsula, and would have obliged them at this time to have retired beyond the Ebro.

On Marshal Soult's unexpected entrance into Placentia, about five hundred of the Legion who had been detached in the neighbourhood of that place, under the command of Captain Lillie, were near being cut off, together with a British detachment of about an equal number, under Captain Tuckett of the 3rd Foot. Some few British soldiers and officers fell into the enemy's hands in Placentia, and some stores.

28. *Vide* Appendix, M.

However these detachments, amounting to nearly one thousand men, were of considerable service in protecting other British stores, &c. from the enemy's foraging parties, which they pushed out in all directions, more especially a large convoy that had been under the charge of Mr. James, purveyor to the forces, who was much indebted for the essential service and protection afforded to him and his stores, by this detachment of our Legion; the British under Captain Tuckett having at this time made a retrograde movement in the direction of Moraleja and Zarza Mayor by night.

Captain Lillie, finding he was unable to effect a junction with Sir Robert Wilson and his own corps, and understanding Marshal Beresford's army to be in motion along the Portuguese frontier, reported to him how he was circumstanced with a detachment of the Legion, in consequence of which he received a communication from the marshal, to endeavour, if possible, to join the British Army across the Tagus, by advancing in the direction of Placentia, which had again been evacuated by the enemy, and to acquaint him and the troops in his rear of any important movements of the enemy: and this detachment was again saved from being cut off the very day they were to have entered Placentia, as it happened, the enemy returned to it with thirty thousand men, of which Captain Lillie receiving timely information, retired upon Sir William Beresford's army. Captain Lillie ordered forty thousand rations to be ready at Galisteo, as he passed, for this Portuguese army, which had the effect of inducing a detachment of the enemy's cavalry, who had advanced there, to retire, and who carried with them this false report to the French headquarters.

Captain Lillie, with this detachment of the corps, remained in advance of the Portuguese army for some days, until the enemy made some demonstrations of attacking Marshal Beresford, when the marshal ordered Captain Lillie's detachment to retire, and placed it under the command of Colonel John Wilson, with whom it remained until this Portuguese army had retired into Portugal, and then it was again united to the main body of the Legion at Castello Branco.

The British and Portuguese armies went into cantonments in the month of September, the former south of the Tagus, and the latter to the north of that river, in the interior of the country, with the exception of the Legion, which remained in advance on the frontier.

Sir Robert Wilson and Colonel Mayne had both obtained a short leave of absence for the purpose of going to England to make a satisfactory arrangement, if possible, respecting the Loyal Lusitanian Legion in Portugal, that corps having hitherto been paid, clothed, and appointed by the British Government exclusively, and not like the other part of the Portuguese Army, to which it had never been attached; but as it was not perfectly understood on what establishment it was to be considered, Sir Robert Wilson proceeded to England for a decision on this important point.

But, in the meantime, while both armies were enjoying a relaxation from the severities of active service, in the interior of the country, and the Portuguese were continuing to be organised under Marshal Beresford and the British officers, it was the fate of the Lusitanian Legion to experience the severe effects of their uncertain establishment; and in the absence of Sir Robert Wilson the privations resulting therefrom. Which might also have proceeded from a little jealousy in a certain powerful quarter, but which was a very ungrateful return for its past exertions in the general service of Spain and Portugal, which undoubtedly had gained the corps the admiration of the two armies in the Peninsula, together with the esteem and gratitude of both these nations.

Surely the Loyal Lusitanian Legion did not deserve to be left neglected on the barren frontiers in the neighbourhood of Castello Branco, which country was exhausted in point of provisions by the different large armies which had lately moved in that direction, or to be deprived of the other advantages which the rest of the Portuguese Army were then enjoying with respect to their comforts, clothing, appointments, &c. &c. which the Legion from its past services equally required.

From these circumstances it is easily to be imagined in what state the Lusitanian Legion naturally appeared after a few months, being badly provided with rations, and in perfect want of all kinds of necessaries, clothing and appointments. Their drilling and discipline oh the British system was likewise at this time much neglected, Marshal Beresford having declined to acknowledge or confirm the appointments of the British officers of the corps who had served with it ever since its organization, and prevented their pay being issued for their services, notwithstanding that the pay of the Portuguese officers and soldiers who belonged to the corps was at this period issued from the Portuguese treasury.

In the month of December following, some information officially arrived, that Sir Robert Wilson had effected an arrangement with the British Government, by which the Loyal Lusitanian Legion was to be placed on the British establishment; consequently a communication was made to Lord Wellington by the government at home, requiring a report from His Lordship, with his opinion of the appearance, discipline, and utility of the corps previous to the conclusion of the arrangements that were at this time promised to Sir Robert Wilson.

It was conceived His Lordship had some reasons for not wishing to interfere on this occasion; and that, from a judicious regard to the feelings of the Portuguese army in general, he chose to avoid making any distinction in favour of the Loyal Lusitanian Legion, and he referred the communications to Marshal Beresford, desiring him, as more immediately connected with the Portuguese army, to make and forward the report of the state of the Loyal Lusitanian Legion at that period, for the satisfaction of the British Government: thus the marshal was afforded an opportunity of satisfying any desire or wishes he might have entertained with respect to the corps, which had acquired the esteem and confidence of the nation long before he arrived to take the command.

The report His Excellency Marshal Sir William Beresford under such circumstances thought proper to make of the Legion after General Hamilton's return from Castello Branco, where he had been dispatched for the purpose of the corps inspection, may be easily imagined; and though the selection could not have fallen on a more able, active, or intelligent officer, yet it was impossible that the Legion could appear in an effective state, after having been so long neglected in every respect.

Such, however, was the report transmitted by Marshal Beresford, that the project of placing the Legion on the British establishment was frustrated, and in consequence of this result, Sir Robert Wilson and Colonel Mayne did not return, which was universally regretted, not only by their own corps, but by the Portuguese nation. After this the corps was brought further into the interior of Portugal, with the few British officers that at this time remained, who were considerably disheartened and dissatisfied after their active services to find themselves so little attended to.

Lieutenant-Colonel Grant, a very deserving and promising officer, was employed by Lord Wellington in obtaining information of the enemy's movements, &c. the others (who were neither permitted by the marshal hitherto to hold their respective ranks in the Legion, or to join their British regiments) were detached about the country, not well knowing what to do with themselves under this extraordinary and undeserved neglect. After some time had elapsed they were gazetted in their respective ranks, and ordered to march with the corps to Thomar, where it received the clothing and appointments which had sometime before been sent from England: here each battalion was recruited and completed to 1000 strong, preparatory to their formation as regiments of Portuguese Caçadores, and an additional number of British officers was attached to them.

Lieutenant-Colonel Hawkshaw commanded the corps at Thomar for some time, until Baron Eben was again appointed in Sir Robert Wilson's place. The Legion now formed part of a division which was formed at Thomar under Major-General Leith, covering the centre of Portugal; and Lord Wellington was opposed to the enemy's corps in the vicinity of Ciudad Rodrigo, which were preparing for the invasion of Portugal, while General Hill's corps was in the province of Alemtejo; and this was the disposition of the allied British and Portuguese armies previous to the fall of the garrisons of Almeida and Ciudad Rodrigo, and the subsequent advance into Portugal of the French army under the command of Marshal Massena.

The Legion continued at Thomar until a corps of the French Army under .General Regnier made a threatening movement on the centre of Portugal, when the first battalion of the Legion was ordered out in advance to take possession of the passes and fords of the River Zezere [29] in front of Thomar, from the town of Punhete on the right, to the Barco de Codes on the left. Here this battalion remained under the command of Captain Lillie until the entire of General Leith's division moved forward to occupy the passes of Saint Domingo, when this battalion joined the advance under Brigadier-General Madden of the Portuguese cavalry, the infantry of which Lieutenant-Colonel Hawkshaw commanded.

At this period the division of General Regnier having made a more determined movement in front of General Leith's division, General Hill's division moved to the north of the Tagus, in order to oppose any attempt of the enemy in that quarter. But the enemy declining any farther threats, the Legion returned with General Leith's division to

29. A peasant of amazing muscular strength became so annoying to the enemy on the banks of the Zezere, that they offered a large reward for his head. This man was accustomed to penetrate the enemy's encampments. He killed upwards of 30 men with his own hands, and captured 50 horses and mules. He lived in a cave in the mountains, but brought his booty to the allied camp to be sold. He was a most determined brave looking fellow, and continued his predatory warfare as long as the enemy remained in his country.

Thomar, where nothing of importance for some time occurred.

The enemy soon after this united the different corps of his army for the purpose of entering Portugal, while the allies made corresponding movements to form a junction for his opposition, which junction was effected conformable to the judicious arrangements of the commander in chief Lord Wellington, in the neighbourhood of Busaco, where the detached divisions of the allied army under Generals Hill and Leith, united to the main body, on its arriving at that formidable position.

Marshal Massena attacked, on the morning of this junction, the allied forces, with what was styled the army of Portugal; and on this occasion the allies obtained a most brilliant and glorious victory.[30] General Leith's division particularly distinguished itself in the engagement, by a gallant charge of the bayonet on a column of the enemy, which had succeeded in gaining the heights on the right, but was instantly routed from it by the gallantry of General Leith and his division, composed of the 1st, 9th, and 38th British infantry regiments—of the 8th regiment of Portuguese infantry, and the Loyal Lusitanian Legion.

The conduct of the Portuguese troops here was eminently conspicuous; the Loyal Lusitanian Legion, and the 8th Portuguese regiment, which had never before been engaged, joined in the charge of the bayonet under the command of Lieutenant-Colonel Douglas and Major Birmingham as gallantly as if they had been veterans. The enemy's attack on the left had likewise been successfully repulsed, the other Portuguese troops equally distinguishing themselves, and especially the 19th regiment under Colonel M'Bean, which charged the enemy by itself in a most gallant and successful manner.—Five companies of the 19th Portuguese regiment, under the immediate command of *Colonel M'Bean,* having made *a charge with the bayonet on the enemy,* which was particularly admired by all the officers of both the armies who saw it, as an act of most perfect gallantry, both on account of the discipline and the courage which these young troops displayed.

After the enemy had been thus repulsed in all the quarters against which he directed his attacks, he did not attempt to renew the engagement, but made a movement to the right along the Sardao road, which winds round the left of the position of Busaco, leading to Coimbra: in consequence Lord Wellington moved the allies from the heights of Busaco across the river Mondego, not deeming it advisable to expose his army to another attack from such superior numbers until his ar-

30. *Vide* Appendix, N.

rival at the lines which were perfectly constructed to intercept any movement on Lisbon; they extended from the Tagus on the right to the ocean on the left, and their natural strength was rendered still more formidable by the assistance of art, strong works having been erected to secure the weaker points, and chains of batteries and redoubts formed on the commanding heights, so well provided with heavy ordnance as to threaten the immediate destruction of any advancing enemy. The French light field artillery could be of little avail against the strength and range of these powerful forts, whose superiority consisted, not only in the weight of their numerous ordnance, but likewise in their being erected on such commanding and formidable situations that no works of the enemy could be constructed, or even attempted in their vicinity.

It is here worthy of observation, that the French army had advanced in full confidence that they were pursuing the British to their ships, and anticipating the laurels they should obtain by driving their opponents into the sea; but on their arrival before these lines,[31] they were struck with universal terror at the idea of attacking them, nor was their dismay lessened by the reflection on the manner in which the bayonets of the allies had been used at the glorious Battle of Busaco a few days before.

Marshal Massena consequently appearing to decline any attack on these lines, remained irresolute in the front of them, while he made a report to Buonaparte of his unexpected situation, and inability to advance, not only from the strength of the position of the allies, but also from the want of provisions, and that he must ultimately be obliged to retreat.

Nothing of importance occurred during the period of the enemy's stay in front of these lines, until he retired by Santarem, having remained until the country was quite exhausted of all kinds of provision, which reduced him to the necessity of commencing a general retreat,[32] which was followed up with such activity and success on the

---

31. *Vide* Appendix, O.

32. On the evening of the first of March a Portuguese boy wag taken in Abrantes with a considerable quantity of hams, tea, sugar, &c. &c. which he had purchased, *but for whom* he felt some difficulty in declaring; on being carried before the governor, and minutely interrogated, he confessed he was servant to the *commanding officer* of the *French 66th regiment*; and that he had been sent to purchase these articles as the French army was retiring to the north of Portugal. He said *Massena* was to review the troops the next day (2nd March); and that the retreat would commence the 5th. The French troops were so reviewed at Montalbo, and the retreat commenced, as he stated, on the 5th of March.

part of Lord Wellington's army and the allies, that out of the French army, composed of one hundred thousand men, on their entering Portugal a few months before, Marshal Massena on his arrival on the frontiers of Spain, could not muster above half that number.

Lord Wellington saw the Legion, and inspected it himself for the first time when attached to the sixth division at Alemquer, in February, 1811; and after a most minute inspection, and seeing them go through some evolutions, march past, &c. &c. His Lordship expressed his surprise at the fine appearance of the corps, stating that he had hitherto been led to entertain quite a different idea with respect to it from the reports that had been made to him; and he particularly admired their fine soldier-like appearance, and observed to Lieutenant-Colonel Douglas, who happened to have the temporary command of the Legion on that day, "that they carried their arms like soldiers, and, in their 'tout ensemble,' looked like veterans."

During the active pursuit of Marshal Massena's[33] army the battalions of the Legion were separated, the 1st joined the 4th division, on its being ordered from the British army to reinforce the troops under Marshal Beresford in the Alentejo:—the 2nd battalion joined the 5th division, and remained with Lord Wellington, which afterwards distinguished itself in the engagement at Fuentes d' Honor, [34] under the command of Lieutenant-Colonel Offley, who was appointed to it from the 23rd Fusiliers.

This 2nd battalion, (*formerly called Baron Eben's Runaways,*) when a column of the enemy manifested an intention of getting round the left of the allied army, engaged at Fuentes d' Honor, by crossing the River Duas Casas, at Aldea de Bispo, on the 6th of May, was ordered to ford the river under the enemy's fire, and dislodge him from a height which he had taken possession of on the opposite side of the river. This service was executed in a most gallant and satisfactory manner; and this battalion afterwards, under the command of Lieutenant-Colonel Hawkshaw, signalized itself most particularly in the south, when joined to that part of the allied army that was entrusted to the command of Marshal Beresford during the absence of General Hill.

This battalion sustained a great loss in the sieges of Olivenza and Badajos:[35] at the latter of which it lost four subalterns and a piquet one

---

33. *Vide* Appendix, P.
34. *Vide* Appendix, Q.
35. Badajos, a frontier town, is the capital of the province, and strongly fortified. It is famous for a bridge built by the Romans over the Guadiana.(Continued next page).

night, by a sudden and unexpected sortie from the garrison; and its loss at the hard contested Battle of Albuera [36] exceeded considerably that of the entire of the Portuguese troops on that memorable day: and this battalion was called forward (previous to the important advance of the 4th division at Albuera.) and attached to the gallant Fusilier Brigade, under the command of the much to be lamented Sir William Myers, who received a mortal wound a few minutes after the success of this spirited advance of the allies, and died thus gloriously, after a short, but truly honourable life.

To the great services of this distinguished brigade, on that memorable day, may be justly attributed the victory of Albuera, for at the critical period of its advance, and brilliant charge, the enemy, having already obtained possession of the rising grounds occupied by the allied force at the commencement of the engagement, were from thence obliged to retreat with considerable loss.

The fate and fortune of that day did not appear previously to promise so favourable a result. The enemy's cavalry had made considerable havoc among the British infantry, which unfortunately had not been formed in a manner to enable those brave fellows to repulse the attempt that was made to break through them, and the French cavalry, aided by the Polish lancers, had dispersed them; and our enemy seemed from these successes to be certain of our defeat. But as the last effort, and only hope, the Fusilier Brigade advanced in line, having its right flank covered from the enemy's cavalry by a Portuguese brigade, which was repeatedly charged by those Polish lancers, who were as often repulsed without touching a man of them with considerable loss.

The Lusitanian Legion fought on the left wing for some time. The enemy maintained his ground on the heights flanked by artillery which kept up a tremendous fire on us, and as we advanced, did considerable execution; but at length, on our coming within a few yards of the columns they gave way with the greatest precipitation, notwithstanding the exertions of their officers to prevent it; and our brave fellows who survived the charge pursued them and drove them

---

It is a bishop's see, and only three leagues from the Portuguese town of Elvas; which garrison, with its dependencies La Lippe, and Santa Lucia, is unquestionably the strongest fortress in Portugal, but the works of the place itself are too extensive. The French, aware of the great consequence of Badajos, have added to the strength of its works; and having fortified it more regularly, have certainly made it a fortress that altogether cannot be considered of little importance in the southern campaign of Spain.

36 *Vide* Appendix, R.

over *three successive hills*, strewing the grounds they fled over with their killed and wounded, after which the enemy did not again attempt to advance.

The Fusilier Brigade and Loyal Lusitanian Legion, which did not exceed three thousand men when they advanced to the charge, could not muster one thousand effective men, when they formed on the rising grounds from which they had driven the enemy. Sixty officers, and two thousand men, including General Cole, who commanded the division, and Sir William Myers, who commanded the brigade, and every lieutenant-colonel and field officer was either killed or wounded.

The enemy commenced a retreat the next day, but did not evacuate the ground he occupied previous to the action for two days afterwards, having left some select troops there to make a front to deceive our army, while he marched off his artillery, baggage, and prisoners to his rear.

This action was supposed to have been the hardest fought of any that ever was recorded in the annals of history, for the time it lasted, and one which threatened, during the early part of the contest, to tarnish the honour of the British arms more than any engagement for the last century; for we had nearly lost the victory with very superior numbers; this never could have happened before in any of the engagements on the Peninsula since the commencement of these campaigns, for in all the other general actions the enemy had considerably the superiority in numbers; and to nothing but the brilliancy and determined courage of the charge made by the light brigade, and the Loyal Lusitanian Legion, is to be attributed this signal victory, which added a lustre, in the room of disgrace, to the British arms, and which shone with such new splendour, that the unfortunate gloom that hovered over the probable result of the previous part of the contest, was lost altogether in the brightness of this gallant achievement.

All the Portuguese staff, and particularly Major-General D'Urban and Lieutenant-Colonel Harding, aided greatly on this memorable occasion, and encouraged their troops while they saw a British soldier stand. It was here the individual bravery of the soldiery and platoon officers so strongly manifested itself by continuing to advance with unabated ardour and steadiness, after their commanding officers had been mowed down, and while the line was raked so terribly by the destructive fire of the enemy's grape and musketry, which appeared only to increase if possible, their enthusiasm, steadiness, and perseverance.

The Spaniards fought bravely at the commencement of the action, and were the first troops who happened to be engaged; however, they were forced to yield, being overpowered by an immense division of the enemy which attacked the part of the line they were ordered to occupy.

It was to be regretted, that the allied troops at the battle of Albuera, derived so little advantage from any plan or *generalship* on the part of the commander-in-chief, while the gallantry of the commanders of the divisions, who were under the necessity of taking things as they found them, fought their brave heroes so successfully, under the greatest disadvantages: and it was still more to be regretted, that the Portuguese troops (with the exception of those attached to the fusilier division,) were not afforded an opportunity of partaking in the heat of the engagement. They would have been of the most considerable importance to the impending fortune of the first part of the day.

A fine body of men, well officered, anxious to engage, must have tended materially to render this victory much more complete, and would have prevented, in a great degree, the immense and irreparable effusion of British blood, for there was not a British battalion in the field that day, that could muster after the engagement one half of the complement it brought into the field, and many could not produce one fourth of their number; and the first battalion of the Lusitanian Legion was the only Portuguese regiment whose loss corresponded with that of the British.

Why were not the Portuguese intermixed with the British troops on this occasion, as had been hitherto judiciously done, and most perfectly approved of on former occasions? Instead of this, they were incautiously formed into a division by themselves, under the command of General Hamilton, (a doubt of whose skill and talent could not certainly be the reason for their not being permitted to join in the heat of the action,) and left inactive spectators of the contest. Brigadier General Harvey's Portuguese brigade, (which formed part of the 4th division, and protected the right of the Fusilier Brigade,) manifested considerable steadiness and discipline on being charged by the enemy's cavalry, which had no effect on them, and proved the service of these brave allies to be worth the trial.

The loss of the allied army in this most sanguinary conflict was computed to be six thousand killed and wounded.

Lieutenant-Colonel Hawkshaw commanded the first battalion of the Loyal Lusitanian Legion through this trying day, and was himself severely wounded.

the commander in chief had it officially notified to Lieutenant-Colonel Hawkshaw, that this battalion of the Legion had so eminently distinguished itself at the Battle of Albuera, and every individual of the corps had acquitted himself with so much gallantry and honour, that they deserved, and should have his thanks in general orders; and he requested that the names of the officers who had survived the day should be given in, that they might be immediately promoted; which strong mark of gracious approbation would have been particularly pleasing to their feelings, if on a former occasion, after the Battle of Alcantara, the same promise had not been totally neglected, and the heroes of that memorable day (all but) disgraced by dark and insinuative abuse. Sir Robert Wilson was not at the Battle of Alcantara.

Thus ended the services of the patriotic and brave officers and soldiers who composed the Loyal Lusitanian Legion, who were shortly afterwards formed into *caçadore* battalions, and their name and uniform so changed that the existence of the corps can hardly be traced in the present Portuguese army.

The corps retained its military character to the last; and as its vital spark was extinguished so soon after the Battle of Albuera, it may be justly said, that it gloriously died there, regaining the trophies of that uncertain day, and maintaining, to the last, its character and renown in its untimely end: and the patriots of Spain and Portugal, and of every power interested in these active campaigns of the allied army on the Peninsula must regret the dissolution of a corps, which not only thus gloriously upheld the noble and warlike spirit of Lusitania in four successive campaigns, but which also was the means in more uncertain and disastrous times, in the year 1808, of proving to the Portuguese nation, and the world at large, that there was enough of this ancient spirit in the body of the Portuguese people to form a regular and efficient army, to be the glory of their country and allies, and the terror of their enemies.

Appendix, A

A SHORT MEMOIR OF THE CELEBRATED PORTUGUESE PATRIOT, THE VENERABLE BISHOP OF OPORTO.

This patriot, whose character is here presented to the public, D. Fr. Antonio de S. José Castro, Bishop of Oporto, and Patriarch elect of Lisbon, is son of Count de Resende, one of the most illustrious families of Portugal, a descendant of the famous Portuguese warrior the governor of India, D. Joao de Castro. To the other titles of his family is annexed that of honorary high admiral.

Early in life D. Antonio applied himself to the studies requisite to qualify him for the church; but renouncing all the brilliant prospects which his family connections opened to his view, he quitted the world, and entered into a convent of the religious order of St. Bueno; an order neither numerous nor rich, and one of those religious societies into which many of the abuses, almost inseparable from such communities, have not yet crept. D. Antonio soon gained the esteem of his brethren by his private virtues, and he arrived at the highest office which they had the power of conferring, being appointed general, or general superintendant, of the convents of his order. This could not long be concealed from the world; and his merits being known at court, he was called by the sovereign from his convent, and appointed, the 13th November, 1793, Bishop of Porto, the second city in rank, population, and riches, in the kingdom of Portugal.

He was assiduously engaged in performing the functions of his sacred ministry, when the people of that city rising against the French, successively deposed and imprisoned three governors appointed in the confusion occasioned by the taking up of arms to expel the enemy, who was then in possession of the country The treachery, real or supposed, of several officers, had rendered the people so suspicious, that there was scarcely any military officer to whom they could look with confidence sufficient to appoint him their leader. The bishop then was thought of; and by the almost unanimous and simultaneous voice of the people, he was proclaimed president of the *junta* for the management of public affairs at that critical moment; and he was, moreover, hailed as the saviour of the country, by all the provinces of the north, and many of the south.

Animated by his example, the Portuguese were preparing to attack Lisbon, and drive the French out of the country; a daring idea, the mere conception of which, without the execution, would confer honour on its authors. But they did not stop at inactive speculations: the Bishop of Porto sent two deputies to the court of England, to solicit arms and other necessaries to put his plans in execution; and at the same time, he spared no labour or application to call forth the resources of the country, as if no foreign succours were to be expected; hereby shewing both his courage and prudence.

General Dalrymple, after the convention of Cintra, new modelled the council of the regency of the kingdom; and no sooner was the form of government established, than the bishop, resigning his authority by a spirited and patriotic publication, submitted to that government; and his example insured the obedience of the people, which otherwise would have been found an extremely difficult task, though the whole of the English Army was then kept in Portugal, perhaps for that purpose alone. Nothing could more clearly demonstrate the good use which he made of his popularity, than his efforts to conciliate the people of Porto to the government in Lisbon; for the inhabitants of the former place openly refused to send money or other effects to the metropolis, and even to allow the bishop himself joining that regency, of which be had been appointed a member.

If the private virtues of this prelate had brought him into the notice of the nation, his public virtue, in his new capacity, endeared him to the people, and his influence was beyond any thing that power or authority could obtain. The almost continued tumults of the populace, who suspected as traitors most of the persons in distinguished situations; the wickedness of those who availed themselves of this ferment to gratify their criminal passions the necessity of arming and preparing the means of defence against enemies enraged at what they called a wanton rebellion: the want of means to obtain provisions, arms, ammunition, and money, rendered the new situation of the Episcopal president most arduous and laborious; he, however, destitute of every resource except the confidence which the people reposed in him, caused a line of defence to be erected round the city, from the Douro to the sea; and in this extensive line were planted two hundred and ten guns.

These works began to be erected in the middle of January, 1809, and in March they received the attacks of the enemy. This expensive undertaking cost nothing to government; and though the exertions of the people in this instance are to be attributed to their patriotism, it is clear that this good disposition would have been of no avail, had such a leader been wanting. In fact, the most indolent could not resist the example of a venerable prelate, rising early every morning, and repairing immediately to the works, animating, cheering, and encouraging the men. He organised the people, dividing them into companies and brigades; appointed officers; exercised them, and, aided by good advisers, did all that could have been expected from an experienced general. When we consider the wide difference between his former profession, and his duties at this crisis, it must be allowed, that his exertions deserve the highest admiration.

The French Army, commanded by Marshal Soult, arrived at length before the city, and prepared to storm it. The French general sent a flag of truce with a summons to the city; and when the Portuguese ceased their fire in order to receive the messenger, the French, with their usual treachery, caused their troops to advance under cover of this deception. The bishop, on perceiving this artifice, immediately gave the word, and two hundred and ten guns of different calibres opened at once upon the French columns.

The bishop refused to listen to their proposition to surrender.

The enemy, however, were successful in their attacks on one of the advanced batteries, and would probably have succeeded in taking it, had not the presence of the bishop animated the people, and the exertions of some English officers of his suite been ably employed in directing the efforts of these irregular troops.

The French were thus driven out of the reach of cannon, and the bishop returning to the city from this successful enterprise, was hailed, as was to be expected, by all the people, with the loudest acclamations, and every possible demonstration of respect. He was to be seen every where on horseback, animating the troops, prompting the men to work, and diffusing confidence wherever he went.

When the French returned to the attack, the insufficiency of the works, which were not quite finished, and the want of regular troops for the defence of such an extensive line, were soon perceived: but notwithstanding: all those disadvantages, the bishop mounted the ramparts, and shared the danger with his companions in arms, many of whom were killed and wounded by his side.

After the entrance of the French into Oporto the bishop was, on the 2nd of January, 1809, honoured by his sovereign with the appointment of Patriarch of Lisbon, and a member of the council of regency, to the universal satisfaction of the Portuguese, who, being witnesses of his merit, were gratified by the justice of his rewards.

Appendix, B

THE PRIVATE INSTRUCTIONS FOR THE BRITISH ARMY ENTERING
PORTUGAL AND SPAIN.

Lord Castlereagh to Lieut. General Sir Arthur Wellesley, K. B,

Sir,

The occupation of Spain and Portugal by the troops of France,
and the entire usurpation of their respective governments by
that power, has determined His Majesty to direct a corps of
his troops, as below stated, to be prepared for service, to be
employed under your orders in counteracting the designs of
the enemy, and in affording the Spanish and Portuguese nations
every possible aid in throwing off the yoke of France.

Troops placed under the command of Lieutenant-General Sir
Arthur Wellesley:—

5th Foot	990
9th	833
38th	957
40th	843
60th	936
71st	903
91st	917
95th 4 Companies	400
R.V. B. 4 Bn.	737
20th Light Dragoons.	300
Total	7816

You will receive enclosed, the communications which have
been made by the deputies of the principality of Asturias, and

the kingdom of Gallicia, to His Majesty's government, together with the reply which His Majesty has directed to be made to their demand of assistance.

I also enclose a statement of the supplies which have been already dispatched to the port of Gijon, for the use of the people of Asturias.

As the deputies from the above provinces do not desire the employment of any corps of His Majesty's troops in the quarter of Spain, from whence they are immediately delegated, but have rather pressed, as calculated to operate a powerful diversion in their favour, the importance of directing the efforts of the British troops to the expulsion of the enemy from Portugal, that the insurrection against the French may thereby become general throughout that kingdom, as well as in Spain, it is therefore deemed expedient that your attention shall be immediately directed to that object.

The difficulty of returning to the northward with a fleet of transports, at this season of the year, renders it expedient that you should, in the first instance, proceed with the armament under your orders, off Cape Finisterre. You will, yourself, precede them in a fast sailing frigate to Corunna, where you will have the best means of learning the actual state of things both in Spain and Portugal, and of judging how far the corps under your immediate orders, either separately or reinforced by Major-General Spencer's, can be considered as of sufficient strength to undertake an operation against the Tagus.

If you should be of opinion, from the information you may receive, that the enterprise in question cannot be undertaken without waiting for reinforcements from home, you will communicate, confidentially, to the provisional government of Gallicia, that it is material to the interest of the common cause that your armament should be enabled to take an anchorage to the northward of the Tagus, till it can be supported by a farther force from home; and you will make arrangements with them for having permission to proceed with it to Vigo, where it is conceived it can remain with not less security than in the harbour of Ferrol, and from which it can proceed to the southward with more facility than from the latter port.

In case you should go into Vigo, you will send orders to Major-General Spencer to join you at that place, should he have arrived off the Tagus in consequence of the enclosed orders; (Letter to Major-General Spencer,) and you will also transmit home, such information as may enable His Majesty's ministers to take measures for supporting your corps from hence.

With a view to the contingency of your force, together with General Spencer's, being deemed unequal to the operation, an additional corps of 10,000 men has been ordered to prepare for service, and which, it is hoped, may be ready to proceed in about three weeks from the present time.

I enclose such information as we are in possession of with respect to the enemy's force in Portugal, a considerable proportion of which is said to have been lately moved to Almeida, on the north-eastern frontier.

You will, no doubt, be enabled to obtain more recent information at Corunna, in aid of which, Lieutenant-Colonel Browne has been ordered to proceed to Oporto, and to meet you with such intelligence as he can procure off Cape Finisterre.

An officer of engineers, acquainted with the defences of the Tagus, has also been sent off the Tagus to make observations, and to prepare information for your consideration, with respect to the execution of the proposed attack on the Tagus. The result of his inquiries he will be directed to transmit, also, to the rendezvous off Cape Finisterre, remaining himself off the Tagus till your arrival.

You are authorised to give the most distinct assurances to the Spanish and Portuguese people, that His Majesty, in sending a force to their assistance, has no other object in view than to afford them the most unqualified and disinterested support, and in any arrangements that you may be called on to make with either nation in the prosecution of the common cause, you will act with the utmost liberality and confidence, and upon the principle that His Majesty's endeavours are to be directed to aid the people of Spain and Portugal in restoring and maintaining against France, the independence and integrity of their respective monarchies.

In the rapid succession in which events must be expected to follow each other, situated as Spain and Portugal now are, much must be left to your judgment and decision on the spot.

His Majesty is graciously pleased to confide to you the fullest discretion to act according to circumstances, for the benefit of his service, and you may rely on your measures being fairly interpreted, and receiving the most cordial support.

You will facilitate, as much as possible, communications between the respective provinces and colonies of Spain, and reconcile, by your good offices, any differences that may arise between them in the execution of their common purpose.

Should any serious division of sentiment occur with respect to the nature of the provisional government, which is to act during the present interregnum, or with respect to the prince, in whose person the legal authority is considered as vested, by the captivity or abdication of certain members of the Royal Family, you will avoid, as far as possible, taking any part in such discussions, without the express authority of your government. You will, however, impress upon the minds of persons in authority, that, consistently with the effectual assertion of their independence, they cannot possibly acknowledge the king or prince of Asturias as at present possessing any authority whatever,—or consider any act done by them as valid till they return within the country, and become absolutely free agents; that they never can be considered free agents so long as they shall be prevailed on to acquiesce in the continuance of French troops either within Spain or Portugal—the entire and absolute evacuation of the Peninsula by the troops of France being, after what has lately passed, the only security for Spanish independence, and the only basis upon which the Spanish nation should be prevailed on to treat, or to lay down their arms.

I have the honour to be, &c.

(Signed)   Castlereagh.

To Lieutenant-General
Sir Arthur Wellesley, &c., &c., &c.

By Lord Burgherst, about to proceed to the scene of action, the following was quickly after conveyed.

Lord Castlereagh to Lieut.-General Sir Arthur Wellesley, July 15, 1808.

Downing-Street, July 15, 1808.

Sir,

Since my despatches to you of the 30th *ult.* marked secret, Nos. 1 and 2, the enclosed intelligence has been received from Major-General Spencer, with respect to the state of the enemy's force in Portugal.

The number of French troops immediately in the vicinity of Lisbon, (so far as this information can be relied on,) appearing much more considerable than it was before reported to be by Sir Charles Cotton, His Majesty has been pleased to direct a corps of 5000 men, consisting of the Regiments below stated:

Reinforcements under Brigadier General Ackland:.

Ramsgate.				Harwich.	
9th Foot 2nd. Bat.	675			Queen's	813
43 ,, ,,	861			20th Foot	689
52 ,, ,,	858			95th 2nd. Bat.	180
97 ,, ,,	769			2 Comp. Art.	200
		Total	5045.		

to be embarked, and to proceed without loss of time, to join you off the Tagus.

His Majesty has been farther pleased to direct, that the troops under Lieutenant-General Sir John Moore, which are arrived from the Baltic, as soon as they are refreshed, and their transports can be revictualled, should also proceed without delay off the Tagus,

The motives which have induced the sending so large a force to that quarter are:

1st. To provide effectually for an attack upon the Tagus; and 2nd. To have such an additional force disposable, beyond what may be indispensibly requisite for that operation, as may admit of a detachment being sent to the southward, either with a view to secure Cadiz, if it should be threatened by the French force under General Dupont, or to co-operate with the Spanish troops in reducing that corps, if circumstances should favour such an operation, or any other that may be concerted.

His Majesty is pleased to direct, that the attack upon the Tagus should be considered as the first object to be attended to. As the whole force (of which a statement is enclosed,) when assembled, will amount to not less than 30,000 men, it is conceived that both services may be amply provided for; the precise distribution as between Portugal and Andalusia, both as to time and proportion of force, must depend on circumstances to be judged of on the spot; and should it be deemed advisable to fulfil the assurance which Lieutenant-General Sir Hew Dalrymple appears to have given to the Supreme Junta of Seville, under the authority of my despatch of —————, that it was His Majesty's intention to employ a corps of his troops, to the amount of 10,000 men, to co-operate with the Spaniards in that quarter; a corps of this magnitude may, I should hope, be detached without prejudice to the main operation against the Tagus; and may be reinforced according to circumstances after the Tagus has been secured. But if previous to the arrival of the force under orders from England, Cadiz should be seriously threatened, it must rest with the senior officer off the Tagus, at his discretion, to detach, upon receiving a requisition to that effect, such an amount of force as may place this important place out of the reach of immediate danger, even though it should for the time suspend operations against the Tagus,

As the force which may be called for on the side of Cadiz, can only require a field-equipment, the ordnance-preparation, which has been sent with a view to the reduction of the Tagus, will remain at that station.

With the exception of the ordnance-preparation sent for the attack of the forts on that river, it has not been deemed necessary to encumber the army at present with any larger detail of artillery than what belongs to a field-equipment, with a proportion of horses.

Exclusive of the period for which the transports are provided, a due proportion of victuallers will accompany the armament, which, with the supplies which may be expected to be derived from the disposition and resources of the country, it is conceived will remove all difficulty on this head, so long as the army shall continue to act near the coast.

The great delay and expense that would attend embarking, and sending from hence all those means which would be requisite to render the army completely movable immediately on its landing, has determined His Majesty's government to trust in a great measure to the resources of the country for these supplies.

There is every reason to believe, from the ardour of the inhabitants both of Spain and Portugal, that so soon as a British army can establish itself on any part of the coast, not only numbers will be anxious to be armed and arrayed in support of the common cause, but that every species of supply which the country produces for subsisting and equipping an army, will be procurable. It therefore becomes the first object for consideration, (if a direct and immediate attack upon the defences of the Tagus cannot in prudence be attempted,) on what part of the coast between Penichè on the North, and St. Ubes on the South of that river, a position can be taken up by the British Army, in which its intercourse with the interior may be securely opened, and from whence it may afterwards move against the enemy, endeavouring, if possible, not only to expel him from Lisbon, but to cut off his retreat towards Spain.

A proportion of cavalry, as far as the means of transport exist, will accompany the troops which can be hereafter increased, according as circumstances shall point out.

    I have, &c.

        (Signed)   Castlereagh.

To Lieutenant-General Sir
Arthur Wellesley, K. B. &c., &c., &c.

The ensuing commission to the senior officers deemed necessary to this command, took place agreeable to their dates.

Lord Viscount Castlereagh to Lieut.-General Sir Arthur Wellesley, K. B. July 15.

                           Downing-Street 10th July, 1808.

Sir,

I am to acquaint you that His Majesty has been pleased to entrust the command of his troops serving on the coasts of Spain and Portugal, to Lieutenant-General Sir Hew Dalrymple, with Lieutenant-General Sir Harry Burrard second in command.

The lieutenant-general has been furnished with copies of his instructions up to the present date inclusive. These instructions you will be pleased to carry into execution with every expedition that circumstances will permit, without awaiting the arrival of the Lieutenant-general. And should you be previously joined by a senior officer, you will in that case communicate to him your orders, and afford him every assistance in carving them into execution.

    I am, &c.

        (Signed)   Castlereagh.

To Lieutenant-General Sir
Arthur Wellesley, K. B. &c., &c., &c.

Lord Viscount Castlereagh to Lieut.-General Sir Arthur Wellesley, K. B.
July 21.

Downing-Street, 21st July, 1808.

Sir,

Ix the event of your deeming it may be advantageous, that the troops now proceeding from England should be disembarked at any point on the coast of Portugal north of the Tagus, I am to suggest to you the propriety of your requesting Sir C. Cotton to station one of his cruisers to the northward of the Berlings, with such information as you may deem material to communicate to the senior officer in command of the troops; and I shall intimate to the officers in charge of the troops proceeding from hence, that they should be prepared at that point to receive an intimation from you of the actual state of things in the Tagus.

I am, &c.

(Signed)   Castlereagh.

To Lieutenant-General Sir
Arthur Wellesley, K. B. &c., &c., &c.

Downing-Street, 30th June, 1808.

Sir,

Referring to my despatch of the 28th inst. I am to convey to you the king's pleasure, that you do proceed, on receipt of this, off the Tagus, there to join the corps under Sir Arthur Wellesley, and to place yourself under his orders.

You will consider yourself, however, as authorised to suspend the execution of this order, in case your corps should be engaged on any service more to the southward, which, in your judgment, it is of importance to His Majesty's interest should not be abandoned.

I have, &c.

(Signed)   Castlereagh.

To Major-General Spencer,
&c., &c., &c.

The orders of Sir Arthur Wellesley have already, in their places, been detailed; those of his superiors are as follows:

Downing-Street, 21st July, 1808,

Sir,

His Majesty having been graciously pleased to select you to serve under Lieutenant-General Sir Hew Dalrymple, as second in command of his forces to be employed in Portugal and Spain, I am to signify to you His Majesty's pleasure, that you do forthwith embark in one of His Majesty's ships, (the *Audacious*) prepared for your reception at Portsmouth, and proceed off the Tagus.

I enclose for your information and guidance, copies of the instructions which have been given to Lieutenant-General Sir Arthur Wellesley, the execution of which is to devolve upon the senior officer for the time being, of the troops assembled off the coast of Portugal.

As it is not probable that Lieutenant-General Sir Hew Dalrymple can arrive for some time from Gibraltar, to take upon himself the command of the troops in person, you will use your endeavours to carry His Majesty's commands, without loss of time, into effect.

You will observe that the operations of the army, are intended to be directed in the first instance, to the reduction of the Tagus; and secondly, to the security of Cadiz, and the destruction of the enemy's force in Andalusia. These important objects being accomplished, it is His Majesty's pleasure, that the senior officer in command of his troops, do act according to circumstances, as the good of His Majesty's service and the advancement of the common cause may appear to him to require, till such time as he receives farther instructions from him for the direction of his conduct; which instructions shall be transmitted, without loss of time, so soon as His Majesty's government, from the movements of the French armies, are prepared to decide in what manner the services of the British troops can be best directed for the annoyance of the enemy.

> I am, &c.
>
> (Signed)   Castlereagh.

To Lieutenant-General Sir
Harry Burrard, &c., &c., &c.

That the necessities of the service were not neglected by the British ministry, will appear from the following note, meeting already the want of cavalry in the British Army for this service.

> Downing-Street, 2nd Aug. 1808.

Sir,

I enclose for your information, intelligence received from Lieutenant-Colonel Browne, and Captain Trant, of the state of affairs in the north of Portugal.

I have directed Brigadier-General Stewart with the 18th Light Dragoons, to call off Oporto for orders, as it is not impossible, if Lieutenant-General Sir Arthur Wellesley should have landed and taken a position in the interior, that you may wish to support him with a cavalry.

I have, &c.

   (Signed)   Castlereagh.

To Lieutenant-General Sir
Harry Burrard, &c., &c., &c.

To Sir John Moore, recently returned from Lisbon, with the only remaining disposable force of Britain under his command, the following were the orders:

         Downing-Street, 21st July 7 1808.

Sir,

So soon as the troops under your orders are victualled, and in a fit state to proceed to sea, it is His Majesty's pleasure that they do proceed, without delay, off the Tagus.

Lieutenant-General Sir Arthur Wellesley, who is now off that port, if not in possession of it, has been directed to transfer to any senior officer who may arrive, the instructions which he has received, in the execution of which it is His Majesty's command, that such senior officer should proceed, as far as circumstances will permit, without loss of time.

Lieutenant-General Sir Harry Burrard is ordered to embark forthwith for the same destination; upon joining him you will place yourself under his orders, in the absence of Lieutenant-General Sir Hew Dalrymple, whom His Majesty has been graciously pleased to nominate to the chief command of his troops serving in Portugal and Spain.

I write this to you in case Sir Harry Burrard should not arrive in time to proceed by the *Audacious*.

I am, &c.

   (Signed)   Castlereagh

To Lieutenant-General Sir
John Moore, K. B. &c., &c., &c.

Statement.

Force under General Spencer.

Artillery	269	
Royal Staff Corps	48	
6th Regt. 1st Battalion	1,020	
29th	863	
32nd	941	
50th	1,019	
82nd	991	
	——	5,151

Force under Sir A. Wellesley.

5th Foot, 1st Battalion	990	
9th	833	
38th	957	
40th	843	
60th	936	
71st	903	
91st	917	
95th, 4 Companies	400	
Royal Veteran Bat. 4 Bat.	737	
36th Foot, 1st Battalion.	647	
45th	599	
	——	8,762

Also a detachment of the 20th Light Dragoons, about 300. With the forces comprised in the preceding statement, and the Portuguese whom he armed, Sir A. Wellesley commenced his march, expecting the arrival of the following force, about to embark from Ramsgate, forming General Anstruther's brigade:—

9th Foot, 2nd Battalion	675	
43rd	861	
52nd	858	
97th	769	
	——	3,163

To embark from Harwich, forming, chiefly, General Ackland's Brigade.

Queen's	913

20th	689	
95th, 2 Companies	180	
	——	1,672

Force with Sir J. Moore.
  English.

4th Foot, 1st Battalion	1,006	
28th	1,087	
79th	913	
92nd	927	
95th	300	
	——	4,23S

  Germans.

3rd Light Dragoons	597	
1st Batt. Light Infantry	930	
2nd	916	
1st Battalion Line	942	
2nd	770	
5th	779	
7th	697	
52nd, 1st Battalion	1,000	
	——	6,631

To join Force under Sir John Moore.

18th Light Dragoons	640	
	———	
		30,262

To join from Madeira one Regiment under the command of Major-General Beresford.

Total.		
Infantry	29,025	
Cavalry	1,537	
20th Light Dragoons	300	
	———	
	30,862	

317 artillery, included in infantry-return of Major-General Spencer's Corps.
The other artillery-returns not received.

French Force in Portugal, as stated by three Hanoverian Deserters, and chiefly confirmed.

In Lisbon and the neighbourhood.

French Infantry.	Total.	
15th Regiment, 2 Batt. .	800	
66th do. 1 do.	800	
70th do. 4 do.	3,000	
82nd do. 2 do.	800	
86th do. 3 do.	2,000	
	———	7,400

French Cavalry.		
3rd Regt. 9th do. Chasseurs à Cheval		2,000

Foreign Infantry.		
Hanoverian Legn. 1st Batt.	800	
Swiss do. do.	800	
	——	1,600

In St. Ubes, (Setuval,) and the forts on the southern side of the Tagus.

(Mostly Italian)		
31st Regt. Chass. 1 Batt.	800	
32nd do. 1 do.	800	
	——	1,600

Troops marched on the eastern Frontiers of Portugal.

86th, 1 Battalion	700	
26th, 2 do.	1,000	
	——	1,700

Foreign Infantry.		
Legion de Neiale	800	
3 Battalions of Swiss	2,400	
	——	3,200

In some Part of Portugal unknown to the Deserters.

47th Regiment, 4 Battalions		3,000

	Total	20,500

3rd Regt. Span. Inf. and 1st do. Cavalry: disarmed at Lisbon, and in prison on board the Russian ships.

150 Russians are landed from each ship, and doing duty in Lisbon. Very little French artillery in Portugal.
General Junot strengthening the Citadel of Lisbon.

(A True Copy.)

(Signed)   G. W. Tucker,
                                                    Lieut.-Colonel.

Appendix, C

THE CONVENTION OF CINTRA.

Headquarters, Cintra, Sept. 3, 1808.

My Lord,

I have the honour to inform your Lordship, that I landed in Portugal and took the command of the army on Monday the 22nd of August, the next day after the Battle of Vimiera, and where the enemy sustained a signal defeat; where the valour and discipline of British troops, and the talents of British officers, were eminently displayed.

A few days after my arrival, General Kellerman came in with a flag of truce from the French general-in-chief, in order to propose an agreement for a cessation of hostilities, for the purpose of concluding a convention for the evacuation of Portugal by the French troops. The enclosed contains the several articles at first agreed upon and signed by Sir Arthur Wellesley and General Kellermann.

But as this was done with a reference to the British admiral, who, when the agreement was communicated to him, objected to the seventh article, which had for its object the disposal of the Russian fleet in the Tagus, it was finally concluded that Lieutenant-Colonel Murray, quartermaster-general to the British Army, and General Kellermann, should proceed to the discussion of the remaining articles, and, finally, to conclude a convention, for the evacuation of Portugal, subject to the ratifications of the French general-in-chief, and the British commanders by sea and land,

After considerable discussion, and repeated reference to me, which rendered it necessary for me to avail myself of the limited period latterly prescribed for the suspension of hostilities, in order to move the army forwards, and to place the several columns upon the routes by which they were to advance, the convention was signed, and the ratification exchanged, the 30th of last month.

That no time might be lost in obtaining; anchorage for the transports and other shipping, which had, for some days, been exposed to great peril on this dangerous coast, and to insure the communication between the army and the victuallers, which was cut off by the badness of the weather and the surf upon the shore, I sent orders to the Buffs, and the 42nd regiment, which were on board of transports with Sir C. Cotton's fleet, to land and take possession of the forts on the Tagus, whenever the admiral thought it proper to do so; this was accordingly carried into, execution yesterday morning, when the forts of Cascais, St Julien, and Bugio, were evacuated by the French troops, and taken possession of by ours.

As I landed in Portugal entirely unacquainted with the actual state of the French Army, and many circumstances of a local and incidental nature, which, doubtless, had great weight in deciding the question, my own opinion in favour of the expediency of expelling the French army from Portugal, by means of the convention the late defeat had induced the French general-in-chief to solicit, instead of doing so by a continuation of hostilities, was principally founded on the great importance of time, which the season of the year rendered peculiarly valuable, and which the enemy could easily have consumed in the protracted defence of the strong places he occupied, had terms of convention been refused him.

When the suspension of arms was agreed upon, the army under Sir John Moore had not arrived, and doubts were even entertained whether so large a body of men could be landed on an open and a dangerous beach; and, that being effected, whether the supply of so large an army with provisions from the ships could be provided for under all the disadvantages to which the shipping were exposed.

During the negotiation the former difficulty was overcome by the activity, zeal, and intelligence of Captain Malcolm, of the Donegal, and the officers and men under his orders; but the possibility of the latter seems to have been at an end nearly at the moment it was no longer necessary.

Captain Dalrymple, of the 18th Dragoons, my military secretary, will have the honour of delivering to Your Lordship this dispatch. He is fully informed of whatever has been done under my orders relative to the service on which I have been employed, and can give any explanation thereupon that may be required.

I have the honour to be, &c.

(Signed)   Hew Dalrymple,
                                                      Lieut.-General.

The Right Hon. Lord Visc. Castlereagh, &c.

Suspension of Arms agreed upon between Lieutenant-General Sir Arthur Wellesley, K. B. on the one part, and the General of Division, Kellermann, Grand Officer of the Legion of Honour, Commander of the Order of the Iron Crown, and Grand Cross of the Order of the Lion of Bavaria, on the other part, each having powers from the respective generals of the French and English Armies.

Headquarters of the English Army,
August 22, 1808.

Art. 1. There shall be, from this date, a suspension of arms between the armies of his Britannic Majesty and his Imperial and Royal Majesty Napoleon I. for the purpose of negotiating a convention for the evacuation of Portugal by the French Army.

Art. 2. The Generals-in-Chief of the two armies, and the Commander-in-Chief of the British fleet at the entrance of the Tagus, will appoint a day to assemble on such part of the coast as shall be judged convenient, to negotiated and conclude the said convention.

Art. 3. The River of Siraudre shall form the line of demarcation to be established between the two armies: Torres Vedras shall not be occupied by either.

Art. 4. The General-in-chief of the English Army undertakes to include the Portuguese armies in this suspension of arms, and for them the line of demarcation shall be established from Leyria to Thomar.

Art. 5. It is agreed provisionally that the French Army shall not, in any case, be considered *as prisoners of war; that all the individuals who compose it shall be transported to France, with their arms and baggage, and the whole of their private property, from which nothing shall be excepted.*[1]

Copy of the Definitive Convention for the Evacuation of Portugal by the French Army.

The generals commanding in chief the British and French armies in Portugal, having determined to negotiate and conclude a treaty for the evacuation of Portugal by the French troops, on the basis of the agreement entered into on, the 22nd instant, for a suspension of hostilities, have appointed the under-mentioned officers to negotiate the same in their names, *viz.* on the part of the General-in-Chief of the British army, Lieutenant-Colonel Murray, Quartermaster-General; and on the part of the General-in-Chief of the French army, Monsieur Kellermann, General of Division; to whom they have given authority to negotiate and conclude a convention to that effect, subject to their ratification respectively, and to that of the Admiral commanding the British fleet at the entrance of the Tagus.

Those two officers, after exchanging their full powers, have agreed upon the articles which follow.

Art. 1. All the places and forts in the kingdom of Portugal, occupied by the French troops, shall be delivered up to the British army in the state in which they are at the period of the signatures of the present convention.

Art. 2. The French troops shall evacuate Portugal with their arms and baggage; they shall not be considered as prisoners of war, and, on their arrival in France, they shall be at liberty to serve.

Art. 3. The English government shall furnish the means of conveyance for the French Army, which shall be disembarked in any of the ports of France between Rochfort and L'Orient inclusively.

Art. 4. The French Army shall carry with it all its artillery of French calibre, with the horses belonging to it, and the tumbrils supplied with 60 rounds per gun. All other artillery, arms, and ammunition, as also the military and naval arsenals shall be given up to the British Army and navy in the state in which they may be at the period of the ratification of the convention.

---

1. The reader must imagine this a dream! but it is too true!

Art. 5. The French Army shall carry with it all its equipments, and all that is comprehended under the name of property of the army; that is to say, its military chests, and carriages attached to the field-commissariat and field-officers, or shall be allowed to dispose of such part of ' the same on its account as the commander-in-chief may judge it unnecessary to embark. In like manner, all individuals of the army shall be at liberty to dispose of their private property of every description, with full security hereafter for the purchasers.

Art. 6. The cavalry are to embark their horses, as also the generals and other officers of all ranks. It is, however, fully understood, that means of conveyance for horses, at the disposal of the British commanders, are very limited; some additional conveyance may be procured in the port of Lisbon. The number of horses to be embarked shall not exceed 600, and the number embarked by the staff shall not exceed 1200. At all events, every facility will be given to the French army to dispose of the horses belonging to it which cannot be embarked.

Art. 7. In order to facilitate the embarkation, it shall take place in three divisions, the last of which will be principally composed of the garrisons of the places, of the cavalry, the artillery, the sick, and the equipment of the army. The first division shall embark within seven days of the date of the ratification, or sooner, if possible.

Art. 8. The garrison of Elvas and its forts, and of Peniché and Palmela, will be embarked at Lisbon; that of Almeida at Oporto, or the nearest harbour; they will be accompanied on their march by British commissaries, charged with providing for their subsistence and accommodation.

Art. 9. All the sick and wounded, who cannot be embarked with the troops, are entrusted to the British Army; they are to be taken care of, whilst they remain in this, country, at the expense of the British Government, under the condition of the same being reimbursed by France when the final evacuation is effected; the English Government will provide for their return to France, which will take place by detachments of about 150 or 200 at a time; a sufficient number of French medical officers shall be left behind to attend them.

Art. 10. As soon as the vessels, employed to carry the army to

France, shall have disembarked it in the harbours specified, or in any other of the ports of France to which stress of weather may force them, every facility shall be given them to return to England without delay, and security against capture until their arrival in a friendly port.

Art. 11. The French Army shall be concentrated in Lisbon, and within a distance of about two leagues from it. The English Army will approach within three leagues of the capital, and will be so placed as to leave about one league between the two armies.

Art. 12. The forts of St. Julian, the Bugio, and the Cascais, shall be occupied by British troops on the ratification of the convention. Lisbon and its citadel, together with the forts and batteries as far as Lazaretto, or Trafuria, on one side, and Fort St. Joseph on the other, inclusively, shall be given up on the embarkation of the second division, as shall be also the harbour and all armed vessels in it of every description, with their rigging, sails, stores, and ammunition. The fortresses of Elvas, Almeida, Peniché, and Palmela, shall be given up as soon as the British troops can arrive to occupy them. In the meantime, the General-in-Chief of the British Army will give notice of the present convention to the garrisons of those places, as also to the troops before them, in order to put a stop to all further hostilities.

Art. 13. Commissaries shall be named on both sides to regulate and accelerate the execution of the arrangements agreed upon.

Art. 14. Should there arise doubts as to the meaning of any article, it will be explained favourably to the French army.

Art. 15. From the date of the ratification of the present convention, all arrears of contributions, requisition, or claims whatever, of the French government, against subjects of Portugal, or any other individual residing in this country, founded on the occupation of Portugal by the French troops in the month of December, 1807, which may not have been paid up, are cancelled, and all sequestrations laid upon their property, moveable or immoveable, are removed, and the free disposal of the same is restored to the proper owners.

Art. 16. All subjects of France, domiciliated in Portugal, or accidentally in this country, shall be protected. Their property of every kind, moveable or immoveable, shall be respected, and they shall be at liberty either to accompany the French army, or to remain in Portugal; in either case their property is guaranteed to them, with the liberty of retaining or of disposing of it, and passing the produce of the sale thereof into France, or any other country where they may fix their residence, the space of one year being allowed them for that purpose.

It is fully understood that the shipping is excepted from this arrangement only, however, in so far as regards leaving the port, and that none of the stipulations above-mentioned can be made the pretext of any commercial speculation.

Art. 17. No native of Portugal shall be rendered accountable for his political conduct during the period of the occupation of this country by the French army; and all those who have continued in the exercise of their employments, or who have accepted situations under the French government, are placed under the protection of the British commanders; they shall sustain no injury in their persons or property, it not having been at their option to be obedient or not to the French government: they are also at liberty to avail themselves of the stipulations of the 16th Article.

Art. 18. The Spanish troops, detained on board ship in the port of Lisbon, shall be given up to the Commander-in-Chief of the British Army, who engages to obtain of the Spaniards to restore such French subjects, either military or civil, as may have been detained in Spain, without being taken in battle, or in consequence of military operations, but on occasion of the occurrences of the 29th of last May, and the day immediately following.

Art. 19. There shall be an immediate exchange established for all ranks of prisoners made in Portugal, since the commencement of the present hostilities.

Art. 20. Hostages of the rank of field officers shall be mutually furnished on the part of the British Army and Navy, and on that of the French Army, for the reciprocal guarantee of the present convention.

The officer of the British Army shall be restored on the completion of the articles which concern the army; and the officer of the navy on the disembarkation of the French troops in their own country. The, like is to take place on the part of the French Army.

Art. 21. It shall be allowed to the General-in-Chief of the French Army to send an officer to France with intelligence of the present convention. A vessel will be furnished by the British admiral to convey him to Bordeaux or Rochfort.

Art. 22. The British admiral will be invited to accommodate his Excellency the Commander-in-Chief, and the other principal officers of the French army, on board of ships of war.

Done and concluded at Lisbon, this 30th day of August, 1808.

George Murray,
Quartermaster-General.
Kellermann,
Le Général de Division.

We, the Duke of Abrantes, General-in-Chief of the French Army, have ratified, and do ratify, the present definitive convention, in all its articles, to be executed according to its form and tenor.

(Signed)   Le Duc D'Abrantes.

Headquarters, Lisbon,
Aug. 30, 1808.

ADDITIONAL ARTICLES TO THE CONVENTION OF AUGUST 30TH, 1808.

Art. 1. The individuals in the civil employment of the army made prisoners, either by the British troops or by the Portuguese, in any part of Portugal, will be restored, as is customary, without exchange.

Art. 2. The French Army will be subsisted from its own magazines up to the day of embarkation: the garrisons up to the day of the evacuation of the fortresses.

The remainder of the magazines shall be delivered over in the usual form to the British Government, which charges itself with the subsistence of the men and horses of the army, from the above-mentioned periods, till their arrival in France, under the condition of their being reimbursed by the French government, for the excess of the expense beyond the estimation to be made by both parties, of the value of the magazines delivered up to the British Army.

The provisions on board the ships of war, in possession of the French Army, will be taken on account by the British Government, in like manner with the magazines in the fortresses.

Art. 3. The General commanding the British troops will take the necessary measures for re-establishing the free circulation of the means of subsistence between the country and the capital.

Done and concluded at Lisbon, this 30th day of August, 1808.

George Murray,
Quartermaster General.
Kellermann,
Le Général de Division.

We, Duke of Abrantes, General-in-chief of the French Army, have ratified, and do ratify, the additional articles of the convention, to be executed according to their form and tenor,

Le Duc D'Abrantes.

(A true copy.)

A. J. Dalrymple,
Capt. Mil. Secretary.

Sir H. Dalrymple to the Commander-in-Chief of the French Army,
Headquarters, Ramalhal, 25th Aug. 1808.

Sir,

The admiral commanding the British fleet on the coast of Portugal cannot agree to the question respecting the disposal of the Russian fleet in the Tagus being in any manner brought under discussion on the basis of the 7th article of the agreement for the suspension of hostilities entered into with your Excellency, with a view to adjusting a convention for the evacuation of Portugal by the French troops.

I feel myself, however, fully authorised to assure your Excellency, that the objection on the part of the British admiral does not proceed from any desire to push to the utmost the advantages which the actual state of the war in this quarter might present to the British forces.

Admiral Sir C. Cotton was put in possession, of instructions from the British Government, respecting the line of conduct to be observed towards the Russian fleet in the Tagus, at a period when circumstances of a nature different from those now existing, induced the expectation that the Russian fleet might be under the necessity of leaving the port of Lisbon, and the

British admiral is ready now to enter on a direct discussion of the subject with Admiral Siniavin on the same grounds.

The intimate connection which so very lately existed between the British government and that of Russia, as well as the personal regard which the British admiral entertains for Admiral Siniavin, leaves little room to doubt of an understanding acceptable to both being the result of a communication between them.

(Signed)

W. H. Dalrymple,
Commander of the British forces in Portugal.

To His Excellency the Commander in Chief
of the French Army in Portugal.

General Friere, to Sir Hew Dalrymple.

Headquarters at Encamacao, Sept. 2, 1808.

Most illustrious and excellent Sir,

Having been informed by Major Ayres Pinto de Souza, by means of a confidential communication, of the articles of capitulation between the British and French armies, which are said to be signed, but of which I have not hitherto received any official copy, although expected; and having heard that the articles do not differ substantially from those proposed in the armistice, respecting which the major made some representations to your Excellency, verbally, by my orders, and also some observations tending to save the honour, dignity, and interests, of the Portuguese nation:

It is my duty to declare to your Excellency, that as I have not been consulted on, or privy to this negotiation, in which I suppose this country is concerned, I consider myself exempt from all responsibility which might have been imputed to me in this transaction.

The present situation of the army here, not admitting me to remain all the time necessary for the conclusion of the negotiation; and perceiving the English columns advancing, without my having any communications of their movements, or indication to co-operate towards entering the capital, I have to expect from your Excellency an explanation on the subject for my guidance.

I must observe to your Excellency, that, in this said capitulation, there does not appear to be any notice taken of the troops commanded by Monteiro Mor do Runo, which are in Alentejo, nor of the Spanish Army which marches in the same province, on the banks of the Tagus, as your Excellency will perceive by the copy of a letter from their general (Don Joseph Galluza,) which I transmit, and who came to assist this kingdom, it possibly may not be the intention liberate the prisoners that still remain in the power of the French army.

God preserve your Excellency, &c.

Bern. Friere de Andrada.

To the Commander in Chief
of the British Army.

(Translated from the Portuguese.)

Memorial on the principal inconveniences which are found in the Convention agreed on between the English and the French Armies for the evacuation of Portugal, wherein is stated minutely those circumstances of the worst consequences as to this country.

Not anything can be more favourable to the French, and consequently more prejudicial to the general cause of Europe, which the British Government profess to aid, than to render the people mistrustful respecting the true motives which actuate that government.

The French will, on all occasions, exert means to excite suspicions against the views of the English government; the conduct of Spain, by having refused, hitherto, to admit undefinedly, British troops into her dominions, notwithstanding the risk she run, proved highly her mistrust in that respect. Amongst ourselves the French partisans have secretly spread this want of confidence, with an intention that, during any moment of ferment, those who came as auxiliaries may be considered as oppressors.

Under such circumstances, nothing can concur more to frustrate the intrigues of the French, than the most prompt declaration of the intentions of the British Government, which we are well satisfied cannot be otherwise than to restore complete, and entire, this country and all its dependencies, to the Prince Regent of Portugal, their faithful ally, who has the unanimous voice of his people; and for whom they will expose themselves to all the evils which might attend this determination, in like manner as they did before they had any assistance from the English, and had no other than their own forces to contend against those of the enemy, their oppressors.

But, at this moment, what is wanting, and particularly interesting, is a declaration of the intentions, which will prevent evil-designing persons from profiting by appearances, to impede the grand and noble designs of Great Britain. Permit me to say that, from the terms in which the treaty is conceived, it may draw into an error, not only the Portuguese, but the Spaniards, and produce the unfortunate and dreadful effect which I have already pointed out; on which account immediate measures should be taken to destroy such impressions.

The British Army cannot, and should not, be considered in this country in any other light than an auxiliary army; and as such they were applied for, by the provisionary government of this country; in like manner it is necessary that it should be still considered, let its strength be what it will, to avoid exciting mistrust, which Mould impede its ulterior progress.

Under these circumstances, any treaty which was to be discussed with the French, should have been done in conjunction with the government of that country, which called the British army to its assistance, or at least, ought to have been done with its particular approbation, should the delicacy of the terms have prevented the arrangement being made public.

Nothing of this sort has been clone, but rather, on the contrary, stipulations are made, which never can be effected by military compulsion and its authority, unless in a conquered country; such as are contained in the articles 16 and 17, and in the first additional article, which stipulate that the garrisons of the sea-ports, the arsenals, and naval forces belonging to the Portuguese, and in possession of the French, shall be delivered up to the British troops, without declaring, at the same time, that such surrender was provisional, and meant to be restored to their legitimate sovereign, nor was it expressed, in any part whatever, that the restoration of the government was the object in view.

Therefore, to avoid the mistrust which such appearances may excite, and which the French will not fail to promote, it appears to be highly necessary, that His Excellency the commander in chief of the British Army should declare, as soon as possible, that the occupying the garrisons, arsenals, and other public establishments, as also the naval forces belonging to this kingdom, was solely a provisional measure, to avoid the contact of the Portuguese and French forces, for the purpose of preventing the effects of resentment, which might lead to acts endangering the fulfilment of the capitulation agreed on. But that, on such danger ceasing, the said objects should be delivered up to the prince Regent of Portugal, or to the government which represented him; and that they should be garrisoned by Portuguese troops, retaining only such English garrisons, as, with the general in chief, might be considered proper for their better preservation, and requisite for the purpose of maintaining good order therein.

As to the guaranteed stipulations in the articles 16 and 17, it appears to be indispensible, that the said general in chief should declare that it never was his intention to prevent or embarrass the taking all necessary measures of precaution against the individuals mentioned therein, to prevent such suspicious persons from prejudicing the public cause, whilst they remain here, and to punish, with the utmost severity of the law, such as might continue to betray this country.

As to the first additional article, the Portuguese general cannot avoid mentioning the impossibility of its execution, unless a just reciprocity shall be established.

It is an indispensable duty to remind His Excellency the general in chief of the British Army, of the necessity of establishing, during the delay of the French in Lisbon, some mode of inquiry into their conduct and actions, and to intimate to them, that for any violence committed by them during that time, against the inhabitants of this country, they will be made responsible.

An equal objection and protest appear to be necessary, and indispensably so, respecting the abuses which may take place in confidence of the articles relative to the baggage, military chests, and the sales of private property with which the said French may involve whatever they may think proper, should this article not be annulled, as a grand disadvantage to us in the capitulation.

I cannot omit remarking the risk to which the said French exposed themselves, and the danger to which the capital is subjected, as also the said French army, by their delay in Lisbon, during the evacuation, from the rancour with which they are looked on by the people of Lisbon; and the inferiority of their numbers may excite some incident, even through the people, which may create an insurrection of a sanguinary nature, within the said capital, and much embarrassment to the English and Portuguese armies, bound on one side by the convention, and urged on the other at seeing Portuguese subjects perish in their sight.

To avoid this risk, it appears to be proper to propose that whenever the first division of the French army may be embarked, the remainder shall proceed to Cascaes, where they can be embarked under the protection of an English division, which can interpose between the French and Lisbon. By which means the imminent danger will be avoided, the evacuation of Lisbon will be expedited, and consequently the robberies and the complaints which might take place will be prevented; but I submit to the government, as it appears proper to do so in all respects.

(Signed)   Bernardin Friere de Andrada.
Headquarters at Encarnacao, Sept. 3, 1808.

The protest was couched as follows:—

Headquarters at Encarnacao, Sept. 4, 1808.
Protest made by Bernardin Friere de Andrada, General Commandant of the Portuguese Troops , against the Articles of Capitulation, conventioned and signed between the English Army and that of France, for the Evacuation of Portugal.

I protest in general, for the want of contemplation in said treaty, of the interests of His Royal Highness the Prince Regent, and the government which represents him, and against all that may interfere with the royal sovereignty, and its authority, or with the independence of the said government, against all that may be contrary to the honour, security, and interest of the nation; and I further protest particularly against the following articles.

Art. 1, 4, and 12.—In the part which determines the delivery up to the British forces, of the places, store-houses, or magazines, and the Portuguese ships, without declaring, in any mode, that such surrender is obligatory, as a temporary act, with an intent, immediately after, to restore them to the Prince Regent of Portugal, or to the government which represents him, to whom they belong, and whom the English forces came to assist.

Art. 16.—Against that part which permits to remain in Portugal the individuals therein mentioned.

Art. 17.—Against that part, which restrains the government of this kingdom from inquiring into the conduct, and punishing by any means, those individuals who have been scandalously disloyal to their prince and their country, by serving the French party; and when under the protection of the English army, they will be screened from the punishment which they deserve, and which would, in future, protect this country from a repetition of their treason.

Additional first Art.—Cannot, by any means, be obligatory to the government of this kingdom without a reciprocal clause, but which is not stipulated.

Finally, I protest against the omission of providing for the security of the inhabitants of the capital and its environs, that they should not be molested or vexed during the delay of the French amongst them, or at least a reciprocity, as inserted in the articles 16 and 17, in favour of the French and their followers; and I here limit my protest, to avoid augmenting a list of them, avoiding to make mention of other subjects of less consideration, such as the cession of eight hundred horses, without attending to their having been nearly all seized by the French in Portugal, and which, consequently, should not have been considered as French property; also the magazines of provisions, furnished at the cost of this country, to which, although in their
possession, they had no real right, as being the unjust possessor of the country.

Bernardin Friere de Andrada,

A few days after was added, through Admiral Cotton, the following still more striking protest from the general of a Portuguese Army, which deemed itself not unimportantly victorious. He at the same time requested an embargo on the transports till they should be divested of the plunder which the French Army contrived to secrete.

Francis Mello del Cunha de Mendonça Menezes, Count of Castro Marino Monteiro Mor of the Council of his Royal Highness, Gentleman of his Bedchamber, of the Grand Cross of the Order of Christ, General in Chief of the Army of the South, Member of the Regency of Portugal, founded by the Prince Regent our Lord, President of the Supreme Junta of the Kingdom of

In the name of the Prince Regent of Portugal, my master, and that of the nation, as General-in-Chief of the Army of the South, posted on the margin of the Tagus, and as a member of the Regency formed by his Royal Highness the Prince Regent of Portugal, for directing and promoting the interests of the nation, I protest, in general, against the treaty definitively made between the English and French generals, without His Royal Highness or his government being consulted; and for the inattention which was paid me, being the commander of an army, which without the aid of a foreign nation, since the memorable 19th of June, on which the Prince Regent was proclaimed in Algarve, found means to drive the enemy from that kingdom, and to pursue him by passing into Alentejo, causing him to abandon all his posts, and march away until my army took up their possession on the south banks of the Tagus, and therefore I protest against every thing that may be contrary to the honour, sovereignty, and independence of the Portuguese nation.

Given at the Headquarters at Azeitaa,
9th Sept. 1808.
(Signed)   Count Monteiro Mor.
To his Excellency Sir Charles Cotton,
&c., &c., &c.

This was succeeded by the following paper on the part of the people.

Sir,

When a general calamity throws into consternation an entire kingdom, it is then that it becomes the grand tribunals which represent the whole nation to interpose their offices to obtain a remedy.

It is evident, that by means of an infamous artifice, under a proclamation of friendship, the French acquired the possession of Portugal, after which they practised scandalous barbarities against religion, against the august throne, against the public security, and that of private individuals, and against the rights of nations.—The ancient and faithful allies of Portugal came to her assistance, and vanquished and overthrew the intruding usurpers; and when we expected a complete satisfaction, it is rumoured that a convention is forming, but which we have barely any knowledge of, as the proclamation of the 10th of September is not satisfactory to the public, and they only know—that in the convention there is no mention made of the three states of this kingdom, that it leaves us without satisfaction for the crimes both against divine and human laws, and without indemnification for the murders, robberies, and all manner of crimes committed by the usurpers.

The proclamation promises to secure restoration of what has been confiscated or seized, but the insults perpetrated against the Portuguese religion, the majesty of the throne, the lives of her countrymen, who have been assassinated, remain unsatisfied by the means.

Our churches plundered of their ornaments, the royal palaces damaged, the royal treasury plundered, and in fine, the people reduced to poverty and misery, so as to render the streets and squares of the capital impassable; nothing of this is taken into consideration, yet those objects are of high importance, as an example not to be passed with impunity, and most imminently so to the religion of the state. The safety of monarchies depends on not suffering their rights to be invaded without punishing the offender, and the consequence of permitting such crimes with impunity, will occasion incalculable misfortunes; by this declaration I discharge my duty with honour and faith to my sovereign, to which I am urged by the officers of this tribunal, imploring of you, in the name of all the people of this kingdom, that you will take them into consideration.

Yet at the same time, they declare their high gratitude to the generous allies who have liberated Portugal; but they pray for a suspension of a convention so favourable to the French interest as it is said to be, the convention being entirely to the prejudice of our holy religion, without a single clause in its favour to bind. All which may be insisted to the prejudice of the crown, without being acted on by the legal representative, cannot take effect. Let those French treat with the victors of Vimiera, who will be indignant at their proposed terms.

The French cannot complain, as they usurped the sovereignty, and therefore they should restore it, as well as the damages, losses, and usurpations, against the sovereign; they insulted our religion, and attacked many of our clergy, whom they plundered; and it is necessary that they should make proper restitution, with all damages and losses, independent of the losses of the dead, the absent, and of those whose misery is seen daily, occasioned by those perturbators of the world.

The convention must be invalid after a continuance of the abuses and hostilities committed in Almeida, by robbing and extorting a contribution to a considerable amount, and the high tribunals of this kingdom cannot consent to the return of the enemy to France, as they even now menace that they will return to destroy even what they leave here.

I am with due respect,

Joze de Artreu Campos,
Judge of the People.

Sir Hew Dalrymple to General Beresford and Lord Proby.

Headquarters, Oeyras, September 6th, 1808.

Gentlemen,

I affixed my signature yesterday to a paper drawn up by Lieutenant-Colonel Murray, which I think contains the most satisfactory proofs that the French have no right to carry off plunder of any sort, at least, while in its original form, and not converted into money; under that interpretation you are to act. I think my own honour, and that of the British nation concerned, that the convention should not be otherwise considered, and I will not listen to any proposal which can compromise either.

I have this day had a deputation from Lisbon, to complain of the depredations even lately committed, and of the shameless and open manner in which public and private property is preparing for removal, and that the fermentation in the minds of the people is coming to the highest pitch of exaltation.

I learn from many and very respectable quarters, that from this, combined with the interpretation the French from their conduct affect to give the convention, the popular rage is little less directed against the English than the French nation, and I may find that the common measures of police, which the French generals themselves are anxious that I should pursue, may be considered as arrangements to secure to the French the fruits of these depredations we have sanctioned by treaty.

Under these considerations, I think it right to suggest to you, the probable expediency of requiring the French to restore to their place, forthwith, the objects of the Arts, and other articles, whether of public or private property, which have been taken thence for the purpose of removal, by that means affording a proof to the Portuguese nation, that we, at least, act with good faith, and are therefore entitled to use the necessary measures, however vigorous, for the protection of those obnoxious persons for whose safety that faith is pledged.

I do not mean by this letter to over-rule those arrangements which, from your local information, and your own judgment, you may have seen cause to adopt: but you are authorised by it, if you see occasion so to do, (clearly explaining the motive to the French general,) to require the demonstration that the system of plunder is overruled and abandoned which I have here detailed.

(Signed)

H W. Dalrymple.
Lieut.-Gen.

Major-General Beresford and
Lord Proby.

General Beresford and Lord Proby, by their active exertions, prevented, as much as possible, the bad effects of the ill-digested Convention of Cintra.

Appendix, D

Extract from General Moore's Campaign

General Orders.

Headquarters Corunna, 16th January, 1809.

The commander of the forces directs that the commanding officers of regiments will, as soon as possible, after they embark, make themselves acquainted with the names of the ships in which the men of their regiments are embarked, both sick and convalescent: and that they will make out the most correct states of their respective corps; that they will state the number of sick present, also those left at different places; and mention at the back of the return where the men returned on command are employed.

About noon the general sent for Colonel Anderson, to communicate his final instructions respecting the embarkation. He directed that he should continue to send the sick men, horses, and baggage, aboard the ships as quickly as possible: but that he wished all the boats to be disengaged at four in the afternoon; for he intended, if the French did not move, to begin embarking the reserve at that hour. And that he would go out himself as soon as it was dark, to send in the troops by brigades in the order he wished them to embark. He continued transacting: business until a little after one o'clock, when his horse was brought. He then took leave of Colonel Anderson, saying, "Remember I depend upon your paying particular attention to every thing that concerns the embarkation, and let there be as little confusion as possible."

He mounted his horse in good spirits, and set off to visit the outposts, and to explain his design to the general officers.

He had not proceeded far on the road towards the position of the army, when he received a report from General Hope, "that the enemy's line were getting under arms"; which was confirmed by a deserter who came in at that moment. Sir John expressed the highest satisfaction at this intelligence; and only regretted that there would not be day light enough to profit sufficiently from the advantages he anticipated as certain.

He stuck spurs into his horse, and flew to the field. The advanced pickets were already beginning to fire at the enemy's light troops, who were pouring rapidly down the hill on the right wing of the British.

The army was drawn up in the order of battle he had planned three days before, and was filled with ardour. The general surveyed them with pleasure, and examined carefully the movements of the French columns. In a few minutes he dispatched almost all his staff officers with orders to the generals at the different points. General Fraser, whose brigade was in the rear, was commanded to move up, and take his position on the right; and General Paget was ordered to advance with the reserve to support Lord W. Bentinck.

The enemy now commenced a destructive cannonade from eleven heavy guns, advantageously planted on the hills.

Four strong columns of French were seen moving from their position. One advanced from a wood, the other skirted its edge; and both were directed towards the right wing, which was the weakest point.

A third column approached the centre; and the fourth was advancing slowly upon the left along the road from El-Burgo. Besides these, there was a fifth corps which remained half way down the hill, towards the left.

It was the opinion of Sir John Moore, that the presence of the chief in command near to the point where the great struggle occurs, is often most useful. (Perhaps Sir John Moore learnt this doctrine from the practice of one of his masters in the art of war, Sir Ralph Abercrombie, under whom he commanded the reserve in Egypt; and though he possessed his full confidence, yet he told the author, that in the hottest fire he usually found Sir Ralph at his elbow.) He probably thought it peculiarly requisite to follow this rule here, as the position of his right wing was bad, and if the troops in that point gave way, the ruin of the army was inevitable.

Lord William Bentinck's brigade, consisting of three incomparable regiments, the 4th, the 42nd, and 50th, maintained this dangerous post. The Guards were in the rear; and to prevent the right being turned,

Captain Napier was dispatched to desire General Paget to bring up the reserve to the right of Lord William Bentinck.

Sir David Baird, leading on his division, had his arm shattered with a grape shot; and was forced to leave the field,

The French artillery plunged from the heights, and the two hostile lines of infantry mutually advanced, beneath a shower of balls.

They were still separated from each other by stone-walls and hedges, which intersected the ground; but as they closed, it was perceived that the French line extended beyond the right flank of the British; and a body of the enemy were observed moving up the valley to turn it.

An order was instantly given, and the half of the 4th Regiment, which formed this flank, fell back, refusing their right, and making an obtuse angle with the other half.

In this position they commenced a heavy flanking fire; and the general, watching the manoeuvre, called out to them, "That was exactly what I wanted to be done."

He then made up to the 50th Regiment, commanded by Majors Napier and Stanhope, who got over an enclosure in their front, and charged most gallantly. The general, ever an admirer of valour, exclaimed, "Well done the fiftieth! well done my Majors!" (Sir John used this expression from having recommended them for the military rank they held. The Honourable Major Stanhope was second son to Earl Stanhope, and nephew to the late Mr. Pitt. The General entertained a sincere friendship for him.)

They drove the enemy out of the village of Elvine with great slaughter. In this conflict Major Napier, advancing too far, was wounded in several places and taken prisoner; and Major Stanhope unfortunately received a mortal wound.

Sir John Moore proceeded to the 42nd, addressing them in these words: "Highlanders, remember Egypt." They rushed on driving the French before them till they were stopped by a wall. Sir John accompanied them in this charge, and told the soldiers that he was well pleased with their conduct.

He sent Captain Hardinge to order up a battalion of Guards to the left flank of the Highlanders; upon which the officer commanding the Light Company, conceived that as their ammunition was nearly expended, they were to be relieved by the Guards, and began to fall back; but Sir John discovering the mistake, said to them, "My brave 42nd, join your commander, ammunition is coming, and you have your bayonets." They instantly obeyed, and all moved forward.

Captain Hardinge now returned to report that the Guards were advancing. While he was speaking, and pointing out the situation of the battalion, a hot fire was kept up, and the enemy's artillery played incessantly on the spot. Sir John Moore was too conspicuous. A cannonball struck his left shoulder, and beat him to the ground.

He raised himself and sat up with an unaltered countenance, looking intently at the Highlanders, who were warmly engaged. Captain Hardinge threw himself from his horse, and took him by the hand; then observing his anxiety, he told him the 42nd were advancing, upon which his countenance immediately brightened.

His friend Colonel Graham now dismounted to assist him; and, from the composure of his features, entertained hopes that he was not even wounded; but observing the horrid laceration and effusion of blood, he rode off for surgeons. The general was carried from the field in a blanket, by a sergeant of the 42nd and some soldiers. On the way he ordered Captain Hardinge to report his wound to General Hope, who assumed the command. Many of the soldiers knew that their two chiefs were carried off, yet they continued the fight undaunted.

General Paget, conformably to his orders, hastened to the right with his reserve. Colonel Beckwith dashed on with the Rifle Corps,— repelling the enemy, and advancing on their flank. They penetrated so far as nearly to carry one of their cannon; but were at length forced to retire before a much superior corps, who were moving up the valley. General Paget attacked this corps with the 52nd and some more of the reserve, and quickly repelled it. He pressed on to a great distance, dispersing every thing in front; till the enemy perceiving their left wing quite exposed, drew it entirely back.

The French then advanced upon the centre, where Generals Manningham and Leith successfully resisted their onset The ground there being more elevated and favourable for artillery, the guns were of great utility. An effort was likewise made on the left, which was very unavailing; for the position on that side was strong. But a corps of French took possession of a village on the road to Betanzas, from which they continued to fire. On which Lieutenant-Colonel Nichols boldly attacked the village with some companies of the 34th, and beat out the enemy with loss.

Light now began to fail, and the French had fallen back on every point; yet the roaring of cannon, and the report of musketry, continued till dark.

The victory was complete, and gained under many disadvantages. The British had been much reduced by the multitude of sick, by the loss of stragglers, and by those employed in necessary duties; and General Craufurd's detachment was now at Vigo, so that not quite 15,000 men were brought into the field. The French also were greatly diminished by the length of the march, the severity of the weather, and their losses in the various defeats they had previously sustained, yet according to the report of the prisoners, their three divisions amounted to full 20,000 men, and consisted, in part, of the same regiments which had capitulated in Portugal. Besides this great superiority of numbers, their position was far more favourable, and their cannon was of much heavier metal, which being planted on the hills, fired down on the British with great advantage. Yet by the daring courage of the troops, by the skilful disposition of the army, and by the manoeuvres during the action, the French were entirely discomfited.

The loss of the British in killed and wounded, was between seven and eight hundred men, and General Hope conjectured that the enemy had lost about double that number; but Major Napier, when a prisoner, learnt from the best informed Spaniards, that the loss of the French was about 2000 men. This was owing to the quick firing and steady aim of the British troops; the French veteran officers declaring, that they had never been in so hot a fire in their lives. Indeed they were often lavish in their praises of the British in action, but observed, that they were much inferior to their own more practised soldiers in marching, and straggled from their corps to a degree which never occurs in a French army. These defects, together with their love of wine, occasioned a most serious loss of men. But to mitigate this censure, it ought to be mentioned, that in the midst of their excesses, no such enormities were committed as other armies are reproached with. The British soldiers were intemperate, and often mischievous, but never cruel.

The darkness of the night made it impossible to pursue the enemy; and General Hope, weighing the circumstances under which the British army was placed, and the reinforcements which were at hand and would soon reach the French, considered that it would be impossible to retain his position long. A succession of attacks from fresh troops must ultimately overwhelm the British. He therefore judged, that the only prudent step that could be taken, was to proceed to embark the army.

At ten o'clock at night he ordered the troops, by brigades, to move from the field and march to Corunna. Strong piquets were left to guard the ground, and to give notice if the enemy approached.

Major-General Beresford commanded the rear-guard, of about 2,000 men, to cover the embarkation. He occupied the lines in front of the town, and Major-General Hill was stationed with a corps of reserve on a promontory behind the town.

The boats were all in readiness, and the previous measures were so well concerted, that nearly the whole army were embarked during the night.

The piquets were withdrawn before daylight, and immediately carried on board the ships also, so that nothing remained ashore except the rear-guard.

The French had no disposition to renew the engagement; but when the morning rose, and they saw that the British were gone, they pushed on their light troops to the heights of St. Lucia.

In the forenoon, (January 17th) they got up some cannon to a rising ground near the harbour, and fired at the transports. Several of the masters were so much frightened, that they cut their cables, and four of the ships ran aground. The troops of these ships were put on board others, and the stranded vessels were burnt. The rest of the fleet quitted the harbour.

At two o'clock General Hill's brigade embarked under the citadel; and during that night, and the following morning, General Beresford sent off all the sick and wounded whose condition admitted of their being removed, and lastly, the rear-guard got into the boats without the slightest effort being made by the enemy to interrupt it.

The whole of this difficult operation was so well conducted as to reflect much credit upon the superintending officers both of the navy and army.

Of the last moments of Sir J. Moore,

As many will receive a melancholy gratification from reading the particulars of the last moments of the life of Sir John Moore, such incidents as are authentic shall be communicated.

The following letter from Captain Hardinge describes his fall:

The circumstances which took place immediately after the fatal blow which deprived the army of its gallant commander Sir John Moore, are of too interesting a nature not to be made public for the admiration of his countrymen. But I trust that the instances of fortitude and heroism of which I was a witness, may also have another effect, that of affording some consolation to his relations and friends.

With this feeling I have great satisfaction in committing to paper, according to your desire, the following relation.

"I had been ordered by the commander-in-chief to desire a battalion of the Guards to advance; which battalion was at one time intended to have dislodged a corps of the enemy from a large house and garden on the opposite side of the valley, and I was pointing out to the general the situation of the battalion, and our horses were touching at the very moment that a cannon ball from the enemy's battery, carried away his left shoulder and part of the collar-bone, leaving the arm hanging by the flesh. The violence of the stroke threw him from his horse on his back. Not a muscle of his face altered, nor did a sigh betray the least sensation of pain.

I dismounted, and taking his hand, he pressed mine forcibly, casting his eyes very anxiously towards the 42nd Regiment, which was hotly engaged, and his countenance expressed satisfaction when I informed him that the regiment was advancing. Assisted by a soldier of the 42nd, he was removed a few yards behind the shelter of a wall.

Colonel Graham Balgowan and Captain Woodford about this time came up; and perceiving the state of Sir John's wound, instantly rode off for a surgeon.

The blood flowed fast, but the attempt to stop it was useless, from the size of the wound.

Sir John assented to being removed in a blanket to the rear. In raising him for that purpose, his sword, hanging on the wounded side, touched his arm, and became entangled between his legs. I perceived the inconvenience, and was in the act of unbuckling it from his waist, when he said, in his usual tone and manner, and in a very distinct voice, 'It is as well as it is. I had rather it should go out of the field with me.'

Here I feel that it would be improper for my pen to venture to express the admiration with which I am penetrated in thus faithfully recording this instance of the invincible fortitude and military delicacy of this great man.

He was borne by six soldiers of the 42nd and Guards, my sash supporting him in an easy posture.

Observing the resolution and composure of his features, I

caught at the hope that I might be mistaken in my fears of the wound being mortal, and remarked, that I trusted when the surgeons dressed the wound, that he would be spared to us, and recover. He then turned his head round, and looking steadfastly at the wound for a few seconds, said, 'No Hardinge, I feel that to be impossible.'

I wished to accompany him to the rear, when he said, 'You need not go with me. Report to General Hope that I am wounded and carried to the rear.'

A sergeant of the 42nd and two spare files, in case of accident, were ordered to conduct their brave general to Corunna, and I hastened to report to General Hope.

I have the honour to be, &c.

H. Hardinge.

The tidings of this disaster were brought to Sir David Baird when the surgeons were dressing his shattered arm. He instantly commanded them to desist, and run to attend on Sir John Moore. When they arrived and offered their assistance, he said to them, "You can be of no service to me, go to the soldiers, to whom you may be useful."

As the soldiers were carrying him slowly along, he made them turn him round frequently to view the field of battle, and to listen to the firing, and was well pleased when the sound grew fainter.

A spring waggon bearing Colonel Wynch wounded from the battle, came up. The colonel asked, "Who was in the blanket?" and being told it was Sir John Moore, he wished him to be placed in the waggon, The general asked one of the Highlanders, whether he thought the waggon or the blanket best; who answered, that the blanket would not shake him so much, as he and the other soldiers would keep the step and carry him easy. Sir John said, "I think so too." So they proceeded with him to his lodgings in Corunna, the soldiers shedding tears as they went.

In carrying him through the passage of the house he saw his faithful servant Francis, who was stunned at the spectacle. Sir John said to him smiling, "My friend this is nothing."

Colonel Anderson, for one and twenty years the friend and companion in arms of Sir John Moore, wrote, the morning following, this account, while the circumstances were fresh in his memory.

I met the general in the evening of the 10th, as he was being conveyed in a blanket and sashes. He knew me immediately, though it was almost dark, squeezed me by the hand, and said, "Anderson, don't leave me."

He spoke to the surgeons on their examining his wound, but was in such pain he could say little.

After some time, he seemed very anxious to speak to me, and, at intervals, got out as follows:—

"Anderson, you know that I have always wished to die this way." He then asked, "Are the French beaten?" which he repeated to everyone he knew as they came in. "I hope the people of England will be satisfied! I hope my country will do me justice! Anderson, you will see my friends as soon as you can; tell them everything; say to my mother—" Here his voice quite failed, and he was exceedingly agitated. "Hope—Hope— I have much to say to him, but cannot get it out. Are Colonel Graham and all my *aides-de-camp* well?" (A private sign was made by Colonel Anderson not to inform him that Captain Burrard, one of his. *aides-de-camp*, was wounded in the action.) "I have made my will, and have remembered my servants. Colborne has my will, and all my papers."

Major Colborne then came into the room. He spoke most kindly to him, and then said to me, "Anderson, remember you go to ————, and tell him it is my request, and that I expect he will give Major Colborne a Lieutenant-Colonelcy. He has been long with me, and I know him most worthy of it." He then asked Major Colborne "if the French were beaten?" And, on being told they were on every point, he said, "It's a great satisfaction for me to know we have beaten the French. Is Paget in the room?" On my telling him, no, he said, " Remember me to him: it's General Paget I mean; he is a fine fellow. I feel myself so strong I fear I shall be long dying It is great uneasiness—it is great pain.— Everything Francis says is right; I have the greatest confidence in him." He thanked the surgeons for their trouble. Captains Percy and Stanhope, two of his *aides-de-camp*, then came into the room. He spoke kindly to both, and asked Percy if all his *aides-de camp* were well. After some interval he said, "Stanhope, remember me to your sister." He pressed my hand close to his body, and, in a few minutes, died without a struggle.

This was every syllable he uttered, as far as I can recollect, except asking occasionally to be placed in an easier posture.

P. Anderson, Lieut. Col.

Appendix, E

COLONEL MAYNE APPOINTED THE GOVERNOR OF ALMEIDA.

Extract of a Letter from Colonel Guard, of the 45th Regiment, dated Torre de Montcoroo, January 9, 1809, to Colonel Mayne, commanding the Fortress of Almeida, &c., &c.

Sir,

In consequence of dispatches which Brigadier General Cameron has just received, he desires me to request that you will, with all possible dispatch, forward the ordnance and hospital stores that are in Almeida to Lamago. The general requests that you will acquaint Sir R. Wilson that he recommends it to him to fall back on Oporto without delay. Should any of the shrapnel shells still remain in Almeida, you will have them completely destroyed; and all stragglers from the British Army must be forwarded to Lamago to wait further orders.

(Signed)   William Guard,
Lieut. Col. 45th Regt.

Copy of the General Orders, dated Adjutant General's Office, Lisbon, January 2, 1809, relative to the occupation of the Fortress of Almeida.

From the increase of expense that must attend the situation of commanding officers of Elvas, Almeida, &c. &e. the commander of the forces (Sir John Cradock) directs, until the pleasure of government shall he known, that the officers in actual command shall receive an extraordinary allowance according to their rank: colonels 24s. *per diem*, lieutenant-colonels 20s. *per diem*; and these allowances to take place from the time of their actually holding the command.

(Signed)   Thomas Reynell,
Lieut. Col. Adj. Gen,

Copy of Sir R. Wilson's Certificate relative to these Orders.

I hereby certify, that Colonel Mayne, of the Loyal Lusitanian Legion, was placed with a detachment of this corps in the command of the fortress of Almeida, from the 5th of January, to the 16th of February, 1809, inclusive, to superintend the transportation of valuable artillery stores, and other arrangements relating to the commissariat and hospital stores, which duty he completely executed with the greatest zeal and to the great advantage of His Majesty's service.

(Signed)   Robert Wilson,
                                                                    Cheffe L. L. L.

*Copy of Lieutenant-General Sir John Cradock's Certificate
relative to these Orders.*

Upon the British troops leaving Almeida, the fort was occupied by a division of the Loyal Lusitanian Legion, commanded by Colonel Mayne, who acquitted himself in that duty much to my satisfaction; and it appears to me, that from whatever source the money can be issued, that that officer has just pretensions to the allowances enjoyed by his predecessors, for such period as he commanded the fortress of Almeida.

(Signed)   J. F. Cradock,
                                                                    Lieutenant-General.

Hereford-Street, Nov. 20,
1809.

Appendix, F

THE CAPTURED MAIL.

Among other valuables in this mail, there was a very handsome gold watch for the Intendant General Danet, of the French Army at Madrid, which now fell into the hands of Colonel Mayne. Captain Danet had formerly been a captain in the French navy, and, after the revolution in France, he commanded the *L'Epervier*, privateer, a very famous fast sailing ship, which made great havoc in the British trade in 1796-97, and in the latter year he captured some of the Quebec homeward-bound fleet, and, among others, the *Adelphi* merchantman, in which were Lieutenant-Colonel Duke, of the 26th infantry, Captain Mitchel, Captain Mayne, and Dr. Miller.

He sent this prize, the *Adelphi*, to Bourdeaux, but he was the means of the release of Captains Mitchel and Mayne, by detaining them on board his own ship the *L'Epervier*, intending immediately to place them on board some neutral that he might meet with on his cruise to convey them to England; he had not time to put this intention into execution; for, looking out for the Quebec fur ships, of (great value,) off the coast of Ireland, he mistook the *Cerberus* frigate, (Captain Drew,) for one of them, and bore down upon her for the purpose of capturing her. It was hazy weather, and when within point-blank shot of her, to his great mortification, he too late found out his mistake, and, after a short and running engagement, Captain Danet was under the necessity of striking to the superior force of the *Cerberus*, and himself and his crew were made prisoners.

The *Cerberus* shortly afterwards went into Cork harbour, and Captains Mitchell and Mayne had the opportunity of returning Captain Danet's liberal conduct; the former by having many connections in that part of Ireland who were civil to Captain Danet on his account, and the latter by obtaining, through the Earl of Camden's court, who was then Lord Lieutenant of Ireland, permission for him to remain upon his parole, and, afterwards, through his relation's, Lady Newhaven's, (Colonel Mayne's aunt), influence with the Marquis of Buckingham, to obtain his immediate exchange and liberation. Captain Danet wrote afterwards from France, in the short peace, inviting Colonel Mayne to pay him a visit, who may, at a future time, have an opportunity of returning this attention, by presenting him with his captured watch.

Appendix, G

Veilla de Cervo, April 2, 1809.

Sir,

I have the honour to inform your Excellency, that I marched, on the morning of the 1st of April, with the detachment of troops, consisting of about 200 men of the regiment of Avilla, 130 of the Legion under my command, 60 Spanish, and 30 Portuguese Dragoons, with one howitzer, and one field-piece, with the intention of surprising or carrying the posts of the enemy at Barbara de Puerco.

When within a quarter of a mile of the village, I detached Lieutenant-Colonel Wilson, with 80 Spanish infantry, and some horse, to alarm the enemy in his rear in case of resistance. The main body was close upon the village before the enemy's sentries perceived its approach; when Lieutenant-Colonel Grant, and Lieutenant-Colonel Don Carlos D'Espagne, *aide-de-camp* to His Excellency the Captain-General, galloped forward with the cavalry, and killed or secured such part of the enemy as could not reach the rocks in the descent of the mountains.

The commanding officer and 16 men were pressed so hard by the detachment under Lieutenant-Colonel Wilson, that they were unable to reach the bridge, and were obliged to throw themselves into a cave at the base of the mountain, which was extremely difficult of access.

The Spaniards and a part of the Legion went down the sides of the mountain, and I posted the remainder of the Legion, with the howitzers, on the height commanding Barbara de Puerco and the road of San Felices; and I brought the guns through the village to the ridge of the path leading to the bridge, from which situation the artillery played with very great effect on the guards ascending the San Felices road and the reinforcements which subsequently descended.

The enemy sent immediately forward from San Felices, where he had 3,000 men, detachments of light troops, who took post on the side of the mountain opposed to us, and where they kept up a very brisk fire, as briskly answered, from eight o'clock in the morning till two in the afternoon, but with considerable loss on their part, from our activity and the excellence of some of our marksmen, particularly some officers and *chasseurs*.

Finding that the enemy persevered in throwing more troops forward, and not having the means or intention to occupy the posts of Barbara de Puerco, especially as I was aware that he could, and did, by single persons, pass and assemble a large force on this side of the bridge, who could divide and turn our position to right and left, I withdrew my guns from Barbara de Puerco to its height, when the Spaniards reascended the hill, and formed on the height about 400 yards from the village.

The troops of the Legion maintained the ground obstinately against the *tirailleurs* of the enemy, who appeared on every side. I gradually withdrew my guns and the Spanish infantry in separate divisions, then the cavalry, as the ground did not admit of its acting; and when the main body had thus descended the hill and passed an intervening open space, extremely unfavourable to cross, under an enemy's fire from the height, I withdrew the troops of the Legion, and, by keeping up a fire from behind a rock that favoured my skirmishers, I passed above the rearguard, without any loss, or the smallest disorder, to the rocky height beyond the plain, where again making a stand in some strength, the enemy halted and retired up the hill.

The troops had directions to halt at Villa de Cerva, where I remained during the night, constantly patrolling to Barbara de Puerco, and where I found that the enemy early at night had, from fear of an attack, withdrawn his forces, leaving only a small guard.

It is a painful circumstance to be under the necessity of citing, even against the enemy, a most flagitious breach of faith and military honour. But it is not only to record a reproach, it is to save gallant officers in the exercise of generous humanity from perishing by similar treachery, that I am obliged to relate, that when informed of the officer and his party being in the cave, at whom the Spaniards were endeavouring to pour fire from every direction, I desired Lieutenant Wilson to offer them their lives on condition of surrendering, and Lieutenant-Colonel Don Carlos d'Espagne accompanied him to prevent the Spanish infantry from firing.

Finding that the communication could not be made on the side of the bridge, these officers, joined by Lieutenant-Colonel Grant and Lieutenant Charles, of the Royal British artillery, passed the bridge, advancing with a white handkerchief, and proposed the terms I desired. The officers came forward and said it was what they wished, and begged Lieutenant-Colonel Wilson to approach nearer. At the instant a volley was fired at him and the rest of the officers, and the fire was continued until they passed the bridge again. Unfortunately, it happened at the moment, the enemy's detachments were descending the hill, so that the complete example could not be made, which such conduct imperiously demanded, but most of the assassins perished, and, I am assured, that only the officer and four men came out of the cave alive.

It is a more agreeable duty for me to add, that, in this expedition, I have had much to praise. All the officers attached to me did whatever bravery and judgment could achieve; and your Excellency well knows, that both must have been required under our circumstances, in the conduct of new levies naturally brave but inexperienced.

This affair has cost the enemy dear, and it is another lesson that no occasion is omitted to attack him, and that he cannot, with impunity, presume in a country where his name is in abhorrence, and where his crimes daily augment the virulence of hatred and the fury of vengeance. Hitherto it is true, that the character of the war, which we have been able to direct against him, has not been on the great scale of military operations, but it is one which has kept him in continual alarm, diminished his ranks, and, I trust, discomfited many of his objects.

It would be improper, at this moment, to notice, publicly, the patriotic zeal and valour of several peasants who accompanied and served in yesterday's affair; but I have the honour to transmit for His Majesty, the Central Junta, their names, and, among so many brave and worthy men, there is yet one to be particularly distinguished for his most gallant conduct.

I have the honour to be,
Your Excellency's most obedient and humble servant,
Robert Wilson,
Brigadier-General.

To His Excellency J. Hookham Frere,
&c., &c., &c. Sevilla.

Appendix, H

Copy of a Letter from Colonel D'Urban,
Quartermaster-General of the Portuguese Army, to Colonel Mayne,
commanding the Loyal Lusitanian Legion, at Castello Branco.

Headquarters, Thomar, April 25, 1809.

Sir,

I am commanded by Marshal Beresford to direct that yon proceed immediately with the Loyal Lusitanian Legion, under your command, to Alcantara.

You will be followed by the militia regiment of Idanhia, which is ordered to march to Castello Branco, and to place itself under your orders.

You will, of course, take with you the guns and howitzers attached to the Legion; and on your arrival at Alcantara, you will make such a disposition of your force as shall appear to you best for the defence of the passage of the Tagus at that place. This is an object of great importance, and you will therefore take every measure necessary to ensure it. The Idanhia regiment marches tomorrow, and will reach Castello Branco on the 3rd of May. I have not sent any specific route for your march from Castello Branco to Alcantara, you will, therefore, of course, march the Legion and the other regiment, by that which shall appear to you the shortest and most convenient.

You will have the goodness to acknowledge the receipt of this letter, and when you arrive at Alcantara, you will report, for the Marshal's information, upon the state of things there, and upon all that you may think necessary for him to be acquainted with.

I have the honour to be, &c. &c.

(Signed)   B. D'Urban,
                                         Quartermaster-General.
P. S. Lieutenant-Colonel Grant, who was on his way to Sir R.
Wilson, has been directed by the marshal to join you, as I am
aware of the great assistance you will derive from his commanding your cavalry and outposts.

Copy of a Letter from General Mackenzie,[1]
commanding in the South of Portugal.

                                         Thomar, May 3, 1809.
Dear Sir,
I find the garrison of Alcantara, which I am happy to learn is
under your command, is a part of the force placed under my
orders by Marshal Beresford, to act with the British troops entrusted to my charge by Sir Arthur Wellesley.
I understand Marshal Beresford has given you some instructions for your guidance, to which I shall add nothing at present;
but you will probably hear from me very soon from Abrantes,
where my headquarters will be after tomorrow.
    I always remain, my dear Sir,
        Your very sincere and obedient servant,
        (Signed)   J. R. Mackenzie,
                                         Major-General.
To Colonel Mayne, Commandant
of Alcantara.

Instructions for Lieutenant-Colonel Grant, Commanding the outposts of
the garrison of Alcantara, at Brozas. Dated May 7, 1809

Sir,
In the event of the enemy moving upon Alcantara in great
force, you will order immediately the 200 infantry, under your
command, to fall back to the heights of Alcantara on the east
side of the Tagus, remaining with the cavalry under your orders
as long as you can in safety? for every information concerning
the enemy's advance. I find the town of Alcantara so thoroughly
exposed, that it is out of the question to take any steps for
its defence; and the greater object being the pass of the Tagus,
it must be abandoned; but should the enemy come forward
in small force, or in any numbers equal to our own, I should

---

1. General Mackenzie fell gloriously at the head of his brigade at Talavera.

122

recommend a skirmishing retreat, falling back upon my force, which shall, in this case, be prepared to give them a very warm reception.

You will patrol on the line of Carceres, towards Aroyo de Puerco, and in the Circle of Alcantara, as your judgment may point out to you, keeping a watchful eye on the upper line of the Tagus.

You will send reports to my head quarters every third clay, of every thing that passes under your command; being careful in procuring and forwarding, immediately, every other information of greater importance.

I have the honour to be, &c. &c. &c.

(Signed)   William Mayne,
                    Colonel, Commanding the Brigade
                                at Alcantara.

Copy of a Letter from General Cuesta to Colonel Mayne, Commandant of the Allied Troops at Alcantara. Dated May 8, 1809.

Most Excellent Sir,

The news that I have received, that 2,000 troops have arrived under your command in the place of Alcantara, has given me the greatest satisfaction, and the more particularly so, as I understand these to be the advance of a large army of British troops under his Excellency General Wellesley, moving into Spain.

I should think Marshal Victor with his army will make a disposition to enter Portugal from Estremadura, to relieve General Soult; and it will give me much pleasure to concert any plans for the impediment of the enemy's movement in the vicinity of Badajoz and Elvas, the former place being now fortified and strengthened in the best possible manner. It is also probable they may try to pass the Tagus at Alcantara, and to move on to Castello Branco in Portugal.

Your Excellency may depend upon every information that I can obtain; and of my determination to pursue the enemy's movement in either case; and to harass them by every means in my power.

I trust your Excellency will have the goodness to inform me of all the circumstances that may transpire for the good of our common cause, and to believe that it will be my greatest desire to render every assistance to the allies, as Captain-General of the Province of Estremadura.

    May God preserve your Excellency! &c. &c. &c.

        (Signed)   Greg. de La Cuesta.

Copy of a Letter from the Supreme Junta of Estremadura, to Colonel Mayne, Commandant of Alcantara,

This Supreme Junta has been very much pleased at the receipt of your dispatch of the 7th instant, in which you inform them of your safe arrival, with the troops under your command, at Alcantara. They beg to send you their most cordial thanks for the energetic disposition that your military skill and sound penetration has made, to put the position of Alcantara in a vigorous state of defence; and they are well persuaded that your presence, and well-directed measures, will prevent the wrongs that Alcantara has suffered, in its weak state, from being repeated; and that the enemy will be repelled with steadiness whenever they attempt to renew their invasion.

The honourable, faithful, and most cordial alliance that so firmly unites the three nations, must re-animate the glorious cause in which all are so much interested; and the *junta*, confiding in your military knowledge, with all pleasure confer on you their full powers of government, for the defence of Alcantara and its dependencies.

God preserve your important life for many years.

                            Louis Maria de Mendoza,

    (Signed)   Juan Cabrera de La Rocha,

        In the name of the Supreme Junta of Estremadura,

Badajos, May 10, 1809.

Copy of an Address from the Junta of Alcantara, to Colonel Mayne, Commanding the Brigade of Alcantara.

The Junta of Government and War of the citadel and town of Alcantara, and its dependencies, in full meeting assembled, having taken into consideration your military and political knowledge, of so much importance in any case of invasion from the enemy, and so useful and beneficial to the Spanish nation and its ally Great Britain, beg leave to name you a member of it, and to request your presence at their councils, when your other occupations will admit of it.

And to beg that you will allow them to distinguish you with

the Cross[2] and Medal of the Junta of the Government and War, as worn by the members, and to present you with them.

God preserve you for many years.

(Signed)   Fernando Maria Pantoza.

Julian Romero Flores.

In the name of the Junta of Alcantara.

Alcantara, May 12, 1809.

Copy of a Letter from the Superior Junta of Castille, dated Ciudad Roderigo, May 12, 1810, to Colonel Mayne, Commanding the Brigade at Alcantara.

The Superior Junta of Castille has received your communication; they are happy to hear that the good and valiant troops that were lately so successfully useful at Ciudad Roderigo, are likely to be the same under your orders, for the defence of our grand cause, at Alcantara. The *junta* have lately received the agreeable news that the Most Excellent General Cuesta has, upon late occasions, been very successful in his attacks upon the enemy, and that his operations are proving very injurious to them.

The *Junta* are very sorry they cannot accord with your request, of placing, under the orders of Lieutenant-Colonel Grant, the cavalry that he had with him in Castille, as they are actually now employed with a division of our army to the great inconvenience of the enemy at Bozan and Ledesma, or they would have had great satisfaction in complying, in every possible manner, with your wishes.

God preserve your Excellency many years.

(Signed)   Ramon Blanco,

Governor and President,

In the name of the Superior Junta of Castille.

Letter from the Bishop of Oporto[3] to Colonel Mayne, of the Loyal Lusitanian Legion.

Most Excellent Sir,

I send these few lines, to assure you of the regard and kind memory I owe to you, and how much I participate in your's

---

2. A Red Cross with a pendant gold medal, one side, "*Al Mérito; de la Junta de Gobierno y Guerra de la Villa de Alcantara*"—the reverse a right-hand and eye with the word "Ciudado"—and on the edge, "*Al Coronel Mayne de la Leal Legion Lusitana.*"
3. Now the Venerable Patriarch of Portugal.

and Sir R. Wilson's welfare, and admire the defence you are making on the frontiers of this kingdom, which I consider of the greatest advantage; and I am glad that you have a part to act in this defence equal to your valour and honour.

I shall profit of every opportunity in which I may have it in my power to shew with what high consideration,

    I remain, &c. &c. &c.

        May God preserve your Excellency.

        (Signed)   O Bispo Do Porto.

Appendix, I

When the French Army, in Estremadura, abandoned the Guadiana, they attempted to cross the Tagus at Alcantara, On the 14th instant, this place was attacked by a division of 10,000 or 12,000 men, commanded by Marshal Victor, Duke of Belluno, in person; they were opposed by the Loyal Lusitanian Legion, with six pieces of canon, the militia regiment of Idanhia Nova, and fifty horse of the 11th Regiment of cavalry; the whole commanded by Colonel Mayne, of the Loyal Lusitanian Legion, whose force did not exceed 1,800 men.

This valiant commandant and garrison disputed the passage of the bridge of Alcantara for nine hours, and then retired in front of the enemy, so much superior to them, with all their artillery, to Lodiero.

The fire of the enemy, whose whole force was engaged, was tremendous beyond conception, although our loss was nothing in comparison with theirs, which at least amounted to 1,400 men.

Lieutenant-Colonel Grant, the second in command, gave the greatest assistance to Colonel Mayne, and these two officers are entitled to the greatest merit for their bravery and conduct on this trying occasion. The enemy's cavalry followed them until dusk; but, by their judicious management, the retreat was effected in the greatest order.

The courage of 1,800 Portuguese, at the Battle of Alcantara, will remain a monument to posterity, and does not yield to the greatest actions of our ancestors.

Return of Killed, Wounded, and Missing, in the Corps of the Loyal Lusitanian Legion, in the Battle of Alcantara.

Rank and File.

103 killed.	143 wounded,	15 missing,
	Officers killed.	

Captain	Vallente,
Lieutenants	Jose Louis de Brito,
	Frederigo de Freitas.

Officers wounded.

Lieut. Col.	Grant, slightly.
Captains	Jeronimo Pereira, badly.
	Felix Mendoza, *ditto.*
	Joachim de Costa, slightly.
Lieutenant	Beltron, badly.

Copy of a Letter (without date) from Sir R, Wilson.

My dear Mayne,

I have had no opportunity of answering your letter from Lodiero, or to congratulate you, Grant, and the Legion, on your distinguished services. "*Hei mihi, quod domino non licet ire tuo!*" Thank the officers and soldiers, in my name, in general orders. The promotion should be secured to the 1st battalion, and I recommend you to forward the names immediately to the Adjutant-General.

I shall be at Thomar on the 5th of June, soon after which I hope to see you, &c. &c.

Believe me, ever yours,

Most faithfully, &c. &c.

(Signed)   R. Wilson.

To Colonel Mayne, L. L. L.

Commanding at Alcantara,

Copy of Marshal Beresford's Orders, Commander-in-Chief of the Portuguese Army; dated Thomar, 27th May, 1809.

Marshal Beresford, Commander-in-Chief of the Prince Regent's troops, takes the opportunity of noticing to the army the conduct of Colonel Mayne at the bridge of Alcantara, where the first battalion of the Loyal Lusitanian Legion defended themselves against a force of 12,000 men, commanded by Marshal Victor, in person. The army will see, that although troops are sometimes obliged to retreat, at the same time they may cover themselves with glory, and merit the greatest praise.

This battalion, and their brave commandant, made a noble defence, and then a firm retreat in the greatest order.

The discipline and subordination of the corps must be good.

The individuals of it do not inquire why they advance or why they retreat, but do as they are ordered, which gives the greatest satisfaction to the marshal, who, approving of their brave conduct, bestows upon them his greatest praise. To Colonel Mayne, Major Grant, and to the officers and soldiers of the first battalion of the Loyal Lusitanian Legion, the Commander-in-chief gives his thanks for their conduct at the bridge of Alcantara; and the marshal requests Brigadier-General Sir R. Wilson to let him know the names of the senior officers of each rank, that he may promote and recommend to the Prince Regent those who so well deserve it.

(Signed)   Brito Mozinho,
Adjutant-General.

After the action at Alcantara, the Prior of the Military Order of Alcantara insisted on taking the Cross of the Order from his own breast and affixing it to Colonel Mayne's, with the verbal communication that the Junta of Government and War, of the citadel and town of Alcantara, had sent off to the Regency of Spain at Seville their strongest recommendation that Colonel Mayne should be particularly distinguished with the Order for his conduct in the action of Alcantara.

Copy of a Letter from Colonel D'Urban, Quartermaster-General to Marshal Beresford's Army; dated Coimbra, May 25, 1809.

My dear Colonel,

I cannot send off a packet to General Mackenzie, without writing these few lines to you, to say that the conduct and gallantry of your people has the highest praise and approbation of the marshal, and all here.

I have sent to Sir R. Wilson all you wished. I am faithfully and truly yours,

(Signed)   B. D'Urban.

To Colonel Mayne,
Commandant of Alcantara.

Soon after these events, General Mackenzie did Colonel Mayne the honour to appoint him to command the van of the allied army[4] moving into Spain. He then returned to the post of Alcantara.

---

4. Extract from Colonel Mayne's Dispatch to Marshal Beresford, dated Lodiero, May 14th.—"With respect to the Portuguese corps under my command, I have only to wish that their gallant conduct may prove them worthy of being joined to a British Army."

IMP:CAESARI:DIVI:NERVAE:F:NERVAE:
TRAIANO:AVG:GERM:DACICO:PONTIF:
MAX:TRIB:POTES:VIII:IMP:V:COS:V:P.P:

IMP:NERVAE:TRAIANO:CAES:AVGVSTO:
GERMANICO-DACICO:SACRVM:
TEMPLVM:IN:RVP:TAGI:SVPERIS:ET:
CAESARE:PLENVM:ARS:VBI.MATERIA:
VINCITVR:IPSA:SVA:QVIS:QVALI:
DEDERIT:VOTO:FORTASE:REQVIRET:
CVRA:VIATORVM:QVOS:NOVÆAM:
IVVAT:INGENTEM:VASTA:PONTEM:QVI:
MOLE:PEREGIT:SACRA:LITATVOR:
FECIT:HONORE:LACER:QVI:
PONTEM:FECIT:LACER:ET:NOVA:
TEMPLA:DICAVIT:SCILLICET:ET:
SVPERIS:MVNERA:SOLA:LITANT:
PONTEM:PERPETVI:MANSVRVM:IN:
SECVLA:MVNDI:FECIT:DIVINA:NOVILIS:

ARTE:LACER:IDEM:ROMVLIES:
TEMPLVM:CVM:CAES:DIVIS:
CONSTITVIT:FŒLIX:VTRAQVE:CAVSA:
SACRI:C:IVLIVS:LACER:II:S:F:ET:
DEDICAVIT:AMICO:CVRIO:LACONE:
IGAEDITANO.

*The following Address Colonel Mayne received from the Officers of the
Loyal Lusitanian Legion.*

The officers of the Loyal Lusitanian Legion, who have had the
honour of serving under the command of the illustrious Colonel Mayne, in gratitude for the distinguished and reiterated
marks of honourable praise which they have received under
his orders, and, for the kind benevolence which he has always
equally extended to the officer and to the soldier, beg leave to
request that he will receive a small testimony of their sincere
regard, which, although unworthy of his merit, they hope he
will consider as appropriate to the occasion.

A sword, with the following inscription:

Outside.

Todos os officials do 1° batalho da Leal Legiao Lusitana a Offerecem ao sen estimado amigo o illustrissimo Senhor Coronel William Mayne, Cavalliero de Alcantara.

Inside.

Presented by all the officers of the first battalion of the Loyal Lusitanian Legion, to their esteemed friend Colonel William Mayne, Knight of the Military Order of Alcantara.

(Signed)

Joao Paes de Sande de Castro, Tenente Coronel.

Duclesiano Cabreira, Major Commandante d'Artilheria.

Filippe Jacob Veloso Horta, Capitao Mandante.

Jose Pinto Sá Vedra e Nevile, Capitao.

Francisco de Paula Rozado, Capitao.

Joao Pinto da Orunha Sa Vedra, Capitao. Joaquim Elias da Costa e Almeida, Capitao Ajudante.

Francisco Joaquim Pereira Valente, Capitao.

Thomaz Joaquim Pereira Valente, Capitao.

Pedro Celestino de Barros, Capitao.

José Estanisláo d'Almeida Rolin, Capitao Quartel Mestre.

Carlos José Francozi, Tenente.

Joaquim Pinto e Souza, Tenente.

Antonio Carlos Pereira da Silva, Tenente.

Federico Cezar de Freitas, Tenente.

Jorge da Fonseca, Tenente.

André Camacho Jorge Barboza, Tenente,

José Bernardino de Sousa Castro, Tenente.

José Cazimiro Pereira da Rocha, Alferes.

José Ribeiro Pinto de Moura, Alferes.

Joao José Gomes da Silva, Capitao.

Brigada de Artilheria.

Manoel José Ribeiro, 1° Tenente,

Cento Marques, 2° Tenente.

Thomé Madeira, 2° Tenente.

Joao Manoel d'Almeida, Alferes.

Colonel Mayne's Answer to the Address of the Officers of the Loyal Lusitanian Legion.

Nothing can be more flattering to the feelings of a soldier, than the approbation of brave men! And the distinguished mark I have just received of yours, is as highly gratifying to me as the satisfaction I shall always feel in reflecting that I have served two campaigns in Spain and Portugal with you, and the brave soldiers of the Loyal Lusitanian Legion!

(Signed)   William Mayne.

Camp near Lo Duero, Midnight, 14 May.

Sir,

I did myself the honour to report to you last night from the camp at Alcantara, of the advance of the enemy, and of our outposts being drawn in.

I retained the cavalry in the town of Alcantara during the night, with a guard of 50 infantry, keeping patrols, videts, &c. to ascertain the immediate approach of the enemy, and as the battle is not always given to the strong, I flattered myself that my letter of last night would have been followed by a more pleasing one than this.

At eight o'clock this morning Lieutenant-Colonel Grant perceiving three columns of the enemy approaching in three different directions, with artillery and cavalry, on the road from Brozas, behaved with his usual circumspection; and having ascertained their strength, 10,000 infantry, 1500 cavalry, and 12 pieces of artillery, some of them 8 and others 12-pounders, very deliberately fell back on the position I had taken, destroyed the passes on either side of the bridge, which had been formed so as to be moved when the cavalry had passed over. Our artillery fired with great effect on the enemy entering the town, covering at the same time Lieutenant-Colonel Grant as he passed with his detachment over the bridge to join me.

Our batteries, composed of 6 guns of the Legion, were formed with fascines, gabions, &c. and calculated to defend the bridge; the infantry were formed on the heights, under the cover of some temporary breast works.

About nine o'clock a very tremendous fire commenced from the two sides of the Tagus, which continued incessant; about 12 o'clock the militia regiment of Idania Nova, not being accustomed to any thing of this kind, and witnessing their officers and men falling and wounded on every side, made a precipitate retreat in a body leaving me occupying the heights of Alcantara, with the remnant of the Loyal Lusitanian Legion, (500 men) and the batteries of artillery.

The French at one o'clock had seven guns all posted, bearing upon our position, and I thought it advisable to put fire to the mine of the bridge of Alcantara, the last act of the munificence and grandeur of Trajan, (Augustus Caesar,) and perhaps so truly venerable, that it ought not to be disturbed, and it only blew up on one side, leaving a free passage for the enemy across the Tagus.

Thus situated, 1200 men of the Idania Regiment having basely left me, I had only one resort, which was, to give Lieutenant-Colonel Grant the command of the main battery, as the only means of preventing the enemy immediately pressing upon me while I effected a retreat. The cavalry of Almeida being reduced by fatigue from 50 to 20, were no cover to me, I therefore thought it advisable to sacrifice one field-piece for the security of the three others and the two howitzers; and finding Lieutenant Colonel Grant very ready to undertake the fighting of the main battery with this one piece, I moved away with the other five, and he did this from two o'clock to three: and I should be doing little justice to his magnanimity, (if I thought myself of sufficient consequence,) to say, that he met with my most grateful approbation. Alcantara can never be named but he with it must be remembered.

Our ammunition being nearly wasted, and our killed and wounded surrounding us, it was absolutely necessary to adopt this mode of retreat with the few brave Lusitanians that were left; and to secure my artillery, the remaining gun was spiked and rendered of no use to the enemy on Lieutenant-Colonel Grant's leaving it to its fate—after he had continued to fire it for one hour to the great deception of the enemy, giving me time enough to pass the plain country, before the enemy's cavalry appeared on the Alcantara side of the bridge of Seguro.

When Lieutenant-Colonel Grant retired upon me, 100 cavalry were close to us, and ready to move upon my infantry, who were much exposed; but by a *ruse de guerre*, shewing only four horsemen in front, and causing a distant firing of the *Caçadores*, they unexpectedly retired, and I learn by a peasant, since to Alcantara.

A painful task now remains for my attention under existing circumstances, which is, to detail our killed and wounded; and although our loss is severe, I am given to understand it is nothing in comparison with that of the enemy's, which has been immense, from the large and numerous body that was exposed to our batteries.

LOYAL LUSITANIAN LEGION,

Killed.—103 rank and file; Captain Valente, a most valuable officer; Captain Jeronimo Pereira, late Adjutant, a promising officer; Alferes Frederigo de Treitas, a promising officer; and Lieutenant Jose Louis de Brito.

Wounded.—143 rank and file; Lieut. Colonel Grant, slightly; Lieutenant Felix Mendoza, badly, since dead; Lieutenant Beltron, badly, and Joachim de Costa, slightly.

Missing.—15 rank and file; 2 subalterns.

IDANIA NOVA REGIMENT

Killed.—2 Captains, 40 rank and file, 1 Lieutenant.

Wounded.—17 rank and file, 1 Lieutenant.

Missing.—4 subalterns, 1150.

I have the honour to be, &c.

(Signed) Wm. Mayne
Colonel of Brigade, and of the
Loyal Lusitania Legion

To Major-General Mackenzie
&c., &c., &c.

P. S. As soon as I can learn the intention and the movements of the enemy, I will write again.

Appendix, K

Letter from Major-General Mackenzie to Sir Robert Wilson, dated Casalegas, 26th July, 1809.

Half past 11 o'clock, a. m.

Dear Sir Robert,

The French have united their forces, (said to be 45,000 men,) and are advancing on Cuesta, who is retiring behind the Alberche; I have been called over here to join General Sherbrooke, and am directed by him to say, that the divisions of the British Army here will also fall back to join the rest of the army behind the Alberche, so that you will make such movements as will correspond with this, and insure the safety of your corps. Everything promises a general action soon.

Always most faithfully yours,

(Signed)   J. R. Mackenzie,

Brig,-Gen. Sir Robert Wilson,

Talavera, and the positions of the respective Armies.

Joseph Buonaparte, styling himself King of Spain, by the 26th of July had concentrated the whole of the disposable French force between Torrijos and Toledo, amounting to nearly 50,000 men, and consisting of the corps of Marshal Victor, General Sebastiani, 9,000 of Joseph's guards, and the garrison of Madrid. And on this day a heavy cannonade commenced soon after daylight, and continued until four in the afternoon, when the commander of the forces, who had rid out at an early hour, returned from the field in high spirits. The action was betwixt the advance of the French and the Spanish outposts, which fell back upon the position heretofore occupied by the enemy on the

Alberche. The Spaniards lost from 3 to 400 in killed and wounded; several of the latter were brought into Talavera in the course of the afternoon.

The cannonade was renewed next morning, the 27th; and the Spaniards, covered by the British cavalry, and Major-General Mackenzie's division of infantry, continued to retire upon the town. As the day advanced, the intention of the enemy to try the issue of a general engagement, became no longer doubtful; and about 3 p. m. his columns, which moved forward after crossing the Alberche with great rapidity, having approached within two leagues of Talavera, the several divisions of the British army were placed in the positions previously chosen, where they remained awaiting the attack. Brigadier-General Alexander Campbell with two brigades of infantry, was posted on the right, near an unfinished redoubt: the Guards, General Cameron's brigade, and the King's German Legion, formed the centre, under Lieutenant-General Sherbrooke; and Major-General Hill's division extended along the rising grounds on the left, flanked by a heavy battery. Major-General Mackenzie, who commanded the advance, had previously withdrawn his troops after the whole of the Spaniards recrossed the Alberche; and this movement was executed with the utmost judgment and ability by that gallant officer. His division formed a second line in rear of the centre.

The cavalry was commanded by Lieutenant-General Payne. Major-General Cotton's light brigade supported the right and centre; Brigadier-General Anson's, and the heavy brigade under General Fane, were on the left. Brigadier-General Howarth commanded the Royal Artillery, and the several batteries were under the superintendence of Lieut.-Colonels Robe and Framlingham.

The ground in front of the British was principally open, but intersected with roads leading to the town, and the bed of a small river, which had been formed by the winter torrents, and was at present dry.

The Spanish infantry, formed in two lines, and supported by the king's regt. of cavalry, were posted behind the mud enclosures of the olive grounds and vineyards, extending from the right of General Alexander Campbell's position to the suburbs and town of Talavera, which they also occupied, having their right flanked by the Tagus.

The Duke of Albuquerque was in rear of the left of the whole line, with the main body of the Spanish cavalry, and Lieutenant-General Don Luis Bassecourt was subsequently placed with about 3,000 light troops in the valley below the left of the British, to keep in check a body of the enemy which appeared in the mountains beyond, which were, however, at too great a distance to have any effect upon the impending contest.

The Spanish Army was commanded by Cuesta, General-in-chief, and the several divisions of infantry were under the orders of Lieutenant-Generals Don Francisco de Eguia, second in command, the Marquis del Portago, Don Rafail Maglano, and Don Juan de Henestrosa.

The French Army, in number nearly 50,000 strong, was commanded by Marshal Victor, assisted by Marshal Jourdain and General Sebastiani, under the direction of Joseph Buonaparte in person.

About half past six o'clock the enemy appeared in considerable force on the heights opposite the centre of the British line, and opened a heavy cannonade of shot and shells, which was instantaneously returned from the principal battery placed on a commanding eminence in the rear of General Hill's division. At the same time the French made a vigorous attack on the left, where, after a most obstinate conflict, they were completely repulsed at the point of the bayonet. The enemy also pushed forward several corps of infantry, supported by a strong division of cavalry on the right, with a view of carrying the town of Talavera, in which object he failed, and was driven back by the fire from the Spanish batteries. The cannonade continued on both sides until dusk.

In the course of the night the enemy made a second assault upon the height; from whence, after gaining a momentary possession, he was dislodged by General Hill, with prodigious slaughter.

At two in the morning the Spanish line was alarmed at all points, by the approach of the enemy's light troops, who were received with a brisk discharge of musquetry, which ceased in about 10 minutes, when the silence of night again prevailed on the field of battle. At length daylight broke upon the contending armies, who were drawn up opposite to each other in the positions they respectively occupied at the beginning of the action on the preceding evening. About six the engagement was renewed, and continued without intermission until eleven o'clock, when the firing ceased, as if by mutual consent, for nearly three hours, during which interval, the French appeared to be employed in cooking, and the British Army reposed on the ground, seemingly regardless of the enemy's presence. It was at this time also, the wounded Were carried off to the rear; and while engaged in this painful duty, the British and French soldiers shook hands with each other, and expressed their admiration of the gallantry displayed by the troops of both nations. The principal efforts of the French throughout the morning, were again directed upon the left; but Major-General Hill successfully repelled every attempt to turn his position, and obliged the enemy to retire with considerable loss.

Sir Arthur Wellesley with his staff, observed the progress of the battle on a height to the left of the British line. From this point he witnessed every movement that was made, and in the midst of the hottest fire issued the necessary orders with characteristic coolness and judgment. Two of his *aides-de-camp*, Captains Bouverie and Burgh were wounded by his side.

At 1 p. m. the enemy was observed bringing up fresh troops and forming his columns, apparently for the purpose of renewing the action; and in fact, about two o'clock, the French again advanced under a heavy cannonade, and made a general attack upon the whole of the position occupied by the British.

The enemy's attacking columns on the right, had arrived within a short distance of the unfinished redoubt, when General Alexander Campbell made a vigorous charge with his division, supported by two battalions of Spanish infantry, and drove them back with the loss of their artillery.

The efforts of the enemy on the left were equally unsuccessful as before, and a charge made by Brigadier-General Anson with the 23rd Light Dragoons and German Hussars, upon a solid column of infantry, although attended wish a severe loss to the former regiment, had the effect of checking their further advance in that direction.

Meanwhile the centre was warmly engaged. Exactly at three o'clock several heavy columns advanced upon this point, and deployed with the utmost precision into line as they entered the plain which lay betwixt the heights occupied by the hostile armies. This was the grand attack; and on the first indication of the enemy's intention, General Sherbrooke gave directions that his division should prepare for the charge. At this awful moment all was silent, except a few guns of the enemy, answered by the British artillery on the hill.

The French came on over the rough and broken ground in the valley, in the most imposing manner, and with great resolution, and were met by the British with their usual undaunted firmness. As if with one accord, the division advanced against the enemy, whose ranks were speedily broken, and thrown into confusion by a well-directed volley. The impetuosity of the soldiers was not to be repressed; and the brigade on the immediate left of the Guards being halted, that flank, from its advanced situation in the eagerness of pursuit, became exposed to the enemy, who had already given way and deserted his guns on the hill in front, until observing this part of the line unsupported, the French rallied, and returned with increased numbers to their attack upon the centre.

Brigadier-General Harry Campbell now gave orders for the Guards to retire to their original position in line, and the 1st battalion of the 48th Regiment was directed to cover this movement by the Commander of the Forces, who saw and provided for every emergency during this tremendous conflict. Foiled at all points, the French withdrew the remains of the columns which had been unsuccessfully opposed to the centre; they however, continued the fire of their artillery, and the engagement, which had been renewed this morning with the rising of the sun, ceased only with its setting.

About six in the evening the long dry grass having caught fire, the flames spread rapidly over the field of action, and consumed in their fatal progress, numbers of the dead and wounded.

A dim and cheerless moon threw a faint lustre over the surrounding objects after the close of day. Small parties were sent out to bring in the wounded; the enemy was employed in a similar manner, and had made large fires along the front of his extensive line.

The troops lay upon their arms this second night, without provisions of any kind—water even was scarce. It was fully expected that the French would renew the attack in the morning, but they retired under cover of the night, leaving in the hands of the British 20 pieces of artillery, and some prisoners. Their rear-guard, consisting of cavalry, alone remained on the right bank of the Alberche at daybreak. The retreat was certainly conducted with ability, and was not generally known in the British Army until long after the enemy had abandoned his position.

This brilliant victory over an enemy so infinitely superior in numbers, has not been achieved without a considerable loss both of valuable officers and men. That of the enemy, however, to judge from the appearance of the field, must be immense.

Soon after 8 o'clock, the British quitted their positions in the field, and again hutted in the wood of Olives. About nine the light brigade under General Robert Crawford arrived, having marched twelve Spanish leagues in the preceding 24 hours.

Information received from a French Officer taken Prisoner.—Report of Marshal Soult advancing on Placentia.

Talavera de la Reyna, 1st Aug. 1809.

Motives of curiosity induced several officers to visit Talavera on the afternoon of the 29th July. The town appeared almost deserted; here and there a few soldiers were walking about looking for the quarters of their wounded comrades. The houses were for the greater part shut up; the inhabitants, previous to the engagement, had tied across the Tagus with their most valuable effects, and had not yet returned.

The French are said to be continuing their retreat. From an officer who was taken prisoner on the banks of the Tagus, the following information has been obtained.

When the combined army arrived in front of Talavera on the 22nd of July;

Marshal Victor's force amounted to	28,000
Joined him from Toledo	8,000
On the 25th two regiments of cavalry, the 14th and 26th infantry.	3,000
Joseph Buonaparte arrived on the afternoon of the 27th, with the Guards from Madrid.	8,000
	———
Total number of the enemy engaged	47,000

Joseph retreated on the evening of the 28th, and slept at Casalegas.

On the 29th his Guards moved forward to Santa Olalla, when they halted for the night.	8,000
Late on that day a division was sent off towards Toledo of	9,000
Killed and wounded on the 27th and 28th, fully	8,000
Remains with Victor	22,000

The above facts stated by this officer, accord with the information received from two dragoons taken with him, examined separately, and also with the intelligence obtained from the *alcalde* at Ceballa, who is known by the magistrates to be a true patriot; to a certainty Joseph is off, but whether to Madrid or Toledo this officer does not know. It is equally certain that a strong division was sent off on the evening of the 29th, to sustain Toledo.

Sebastiani had a command in the battle, and Marshal Jourdain remained with Joseph Buonaparte until he quitted the field. Victor commanded under the immediate direction of Joseph.

The French Army is in the greatest distress for provisions, and the troops have had little bread from the day they were first driven out of Talavera, and none from the 27th until the 31st, when 4,000 pounds of biscuit arrived from Madrid, and a further supply was expected, but this is supposed to have been taken. The whole of the French from Victor down to the lowest soldier, are discontented with the war in Spain, and all wish to return to their own country.

On the arrival of Joseph on the 27th, he publicly reproached Victor for not having beaten or taken the British and Spanish armies already, and assured the army that this should be done on the 28th. He was seen on the evening of that day retiring from the field, the picture of melancholy and disappointment.

This prisoner heard Victor say, on the afternoon of the 28th, that he felt himself abandoned by Soult. On the 30th it was known in the French Army, that the latter was coming round by Placentia with 12,000 men.

When the troops came from Toledo to join Victor, there were only 1500 left in that city, and Joseph withdrew the whole of the garrison from Madrid, except about 3,000 men, of whom a part were stationed in the port of El Retiro.

It caused much consternation in the French Army to hear, during the engagement, that Toledo was bombarded by Venegas, (whose operations were restrained by an order of the Junta,) and that the British had been reinforced by General Crawford's division.

General Morlot was killed, and Lapisse received a mortal wound on the 28th, of which he died the next day. An immense number of colonels and field officers were killed and wounded, and the oldest soldiers in the French Army declared the day after the action, that they had never seen more determined fighting; and all agreed, that in the war with Spain this was the first time they had met with soldiers.

They wondered where the Spaniards were; as their position was covered with wood, our allies were not seen by the French.

The sick and wounded of the army are in a shocking state; and this prisoner thinks the retreat is suspended to give as much time as possible to send away the wounded, which is almost impracticable, as they have scarcely any means of conveyance.

All letters from France are opened by order of Joseph Buonaparte, and those burned which contain bad news. The French Army, however, has heard of Napoleon's defeat in Austria.

The report of this day is, that Marshal Soult is advancing with 12,000 or 15,000 men on Placentia, from which he was only 10 leagues distant on the 30th *ultimo*.

Appendix, L

THE LEGION OBLIGE THE FRENCH TO RETREAT TO MAQUEDA

(From the *Moniteur*)

Paris, Sept. 27, 1809.

Report to the King, commanding the French Armies in Spain.

Sire,

Your Majesty has ordered me to draw up a general report of the operations of the army, from the 23rd of July last to the 15th instant. I have strictly complied with your commands.

Before I give Your Majesty an account of the marches of the different corps of the army, and the brilliant actions which have conferred glory on the Imperial troops, I think it necessary, for the elucidation of my report, to describe the position of the respective corps of the Imperial army, and that of the hostile armies, on the 20th of July.

POSITION OF THE IMPERIAL ARMY, AND OF THE ENEMY'S ARMY, ON THE 20TH JULY, 1809.

At this time the 4th corps, commanded by General Sebastiani, was posted at Consuegra and Madrilejos, watching the army of Venegas, 30,000 strong. This army occupied Manzanares and Daymiel, and had its advanced posts on the Guadiana.

The 1st corps, commanded by Marshal the Duke of Belluno, was posted on the left bank of the Alberche, in front of Casalegas, covering the pass from Talavera towards Madrid. The advanced guard of this corps of the army occupied Talavera de la Reyna.

Marshal the Duke of Belluno watched the army of Cuesta, 30,000 strong, which had crossed to the right bank of the Tagus, by a bridge thrown over that river at Almaraz, and by the bridge of Arzobispo.

Your Majesty had received orders from his Imperial and Royal

Majesty, directing that the Duke of Dalmatia should unite, under his command, the 2nd, 5th, and 6th corps, consisting of 80 battalions and 30 squadrons, amounting to upwards of 60,000 effective men; that he should march against the English, should seek them out wherever they might be, and engage

Meanwhile the 2nd corps still occupied Salamanca and Zamora.

The 5th corps was in Valladolid and its environs, and the 6th occupied Benevente, Astorga, and Leon. The latter corps had in its front the troops commanded by La Romana, and the insurgents of Galicia and the Asturias,

Independently of the armies of the insurgents, report announced that an English Army, 30,000 strong, was assembling in the environs of Placentia, under the command of General Wellesley.

On the 22nd July, your Majesty received intelligence from Marshal the Duke of Belluno, that the English army, under the command of General Wellesley, had formed a junction between the Tagus and the Tietar, with the army of Cuesta, and that this combined force was on its march towards Talavera; while a corps of eight or ten thousand men, commanded by General Wilson, was advancing towards Escalona, along the right bank of the Alberche. The danger was imminent; and it was necessary to take decided measures.

The same day, (22nd,) your Majesty sent orders to Marshal the Duke of Dalmatia to unite speedily, at Salamanca, the three corps of the army under his command, and to advance rapidly to Placentia, in order to break the line of operation of the hostile army. You, at the same time, ordered General Sebastiani to proceed, by forced marches, with the 4th corps, from Madrilejos to Toledo. Your Majesty left Madrid in the night between the 22nd and 23rd, with your reserve composed of the Royal Guard, and the brigade of General Oudinot, formed of the 12th regiment of infantry, the 51st regiment of the line, and the 27th regiment of horse *chasseurs*. The command of this reserve was entrusted to the General of Division Dessolles.

In proceeding to Naval-Carnero, your Majesty had a two-fold object: to check the march of General Wilson, who endeavoured to get in the rear of the 1st corps, by Escalona; and to form a junction with Marshal the Duke of Belluno, with a view to enable him to keep the enemy in check till the junction of the 4th corps, and till the result of the march of Marshal the Duke of Dalmatia should be ascertained.

Meanwhile, in the evening of the 23rd, Marshal the Duke of Belluno informed your Majesty, that, on the 22nd, the advanced guard of his corps of the army had been obliged to quit Talavera de la Reyna, and to retire along the left bank of the Alberche; that he was certain he should be attacked on the 24th, by the combined armies of the English and Cuesta; and that, unwilling to hazard the 1st corps against such a superior force, he should march in the night between the 23rd and 24th, and proceed in two days to the left bank of the Guadarama, at its conflux with the Tagus, near Toledo, in order to effect a junction with the 4th corps. Your Majesty will highly approve the movement of Marshal the Duke of Belluno; for, if that Marshal had retreated upon Naval-Carnero, instead of retiring to Toledo, the junction of the 1st and 4th corps would have been rendered extremely difficult, and perhaps even impossible.

It is likewise very certain, that Marshal the Duke of Belluno had formed a correct judgment of the designs of the enemy. Orders found upon the officers have proved, that the 1st corps was to have been attacked, on the morning of the 24th, by the English Army and that of Cuesta, in its position on the Alberche, whilst Wilson's corps was to have endeavoured to cut off its retreat towards Madrid, by advancing from Escalona upon Naval-Carnero.

Your Majesty, on receiving the letter of Marshal the Duke of Belluno, took the resolution of proceeding also towards Toledo, with your reserve, in order to form a junction with the 1st and 4th corps, and to present to the enemy a body, imposing, not from its numbers, but from its valour.

On the 24th, your Majesty advanced with your reserve to Cavanara, three leagues from Toledo. The next day, the 25th, you fixed your headquarters at Bargas.

The same day, General Sebastiani, after ably disguising his movements from Venegas, arrived with the 4th corps at Toledo. Lastly, the 1st corps had taken a position on the left bank of the Guadarama; so that all the troops which it was in your Majesty's power to oppose to the enemy, were united.

Your Majesty ordered a detachment to be left at Toledo, to guard that city and the bridges.

On the 26th, your Majesty ordered the whole army to pass over the bridge of Guadarama, and advance upon Torrijos. The first corps opened the march. General Latour Maubourg commanded the whole of the cavalry of the 1st corps, to which your Majesty had joined the division of light cavalry, under General Merlin, which had previously been attached to the 4th corps.

On the 25th, Cuesta's army took up a position at Santa Olalla; it was to continue its march on the 26th, to advance upon Toledo, with a view to attempt a junction with Venegas. The English Army had not yet quitted Talavera, but had pushed its advanced guard to Casalegas, on the left bank of the Alberche. Wilson's corps had continued its movement, and had pushed its advanced posts to Naval-Carnero.

Then follows the account of the Battle of Talavera, during which battle the Legion had marched from Naval-Carnero and the neighbourhood of Mostoloz, to rejoin Lord Wellington, by his order received on the morning of the 27th; but the French Army intervening, they were lodged, during that battle, in a wood half a mile from Casalegas, the headquarters of Joseph, and immediately in the rear of the enemy's army. After that battle *they voluntarily re-advanced to remove the French from their position*, and thus the enemy certifies the success of that very interesting operation.

On the 31st, the 4th corps and the reserve rested.

In the night between the 31st July and the 1st August, Marshal the Duke of Belluno informed your Majesty, that he was apprised that the English army still remained at Talavera, with that of Cuesta; *and that a Portuguese column had put itself in motion among the mountains, to turn the right of the first corps; he added, that, in consequence of this intelligence, he should quit his position, and retire upon Maqueda.* On the other hand, your Majesty was informed, that Venegas had withdrawn from before Toledo part of his troops who had attacked that place; that he was concentrating his forces upon Aranjuez, and that he manifested an intention of marching towards Madrid. Your Majesty then thought fit to post the 4th corps and the reserve in such a manner, as to enable them to advance rapidly either upon the 1st corps, to impede the march of the combined and discomfited army, or upon Venegas, if his army attempted to march towards Madrid. Your Majesty, in consequence, ordered that a garrison should be left at Toledo, under the command of the Adjutant-Commandant Mocquerey, whom you appointed governor of that place, and that the reserve and the 4th corps should march, and take up a position, on the 1st August, at Illescas. General Milhaud received orders to send out strong parties of cavalry in the direction of Valdemoro, to watch the motions of the army of Venegas. Venegas caused his advanced posts to fall back, and merely kept an advanced guard on the right bank of the Tagus, in front of Aranjuez.—August the 2nd and 3rd, the 4th corps and the reserve remained in their positions.

August the 2nd, the Duke of Belluno informed your Majesty by letter that the enemy appeared in the direction of Escalona, on the right bank of the Alberche; that the parties which had been sent from Escalona to Numbella had been attacked by some troops of the enemy's cavalry.[1]

The marshal added, that he had sent two regiments of dragoons with orders to observe what was passing there; and that if he learned that the enemy was directing his course to that point, he would retire upon Mostoloz;[2] but that, in the contrary case, he should remain at Maqueda.

The report of the Duke of Belluno did not announce the march of the combined army: it related only to Wilson's corps, which manifested an intention of annoying the right of the first corps. Your Majesty then thought that it was not yet time to join the 1st corps with the 4th, and the reserve; but with a view to facilitate their junction, if it should be found necessary, you proceeded with your reserve, in the night between the 3rd and 4th of August, to Mostoloz, and the 4th corps remained at Illescas, to continue to watch the army of Venegas.

Fresh reports addressed to your Majesty on the 4th, by Marshal the Duke of Belluno, stated, that the combined army had not yet advanced, that it had only pushed on some cavalry towards Santa Olalla, and that the corps which was at Numbella was not supported by a considerable body, as it bad been reported that it was. The marshal added, that he had made arrangements for attacking General Wilson, at Numbella, on the morning of the 5th.

Your Majesty left Mostoloz in the night between the 4th and 5th, to proceed towards Valdemoro. General Sebastiani received orders to advance likewise with the 4th corps, from Illescas to Valdemoro, where your Majesty immediately directed it to pursue the road of Aranjuez, in order to attack the advanced guard of the army of Venegas, which was on the right bank of the Tagus, between that river and the Tajona. Your Majesty's orders were executed. The advanced guard of Venegas, 10,000 strong, was routed, and obliged to fall back on the left bank of the Tagus. The enemy destroyed his bridges. On the 6th, the 4th corps

---

1. The mounted officers and 14 dragoons, attached to the Legion, which had no other cavalry at that time.
2. Behind the Guadarama River, three leagues from Madrid.

and the reserve remained in their position.

Marshal the Duke of Belluno, by letter of the 5th August, acquaint-ed your Majesty, that Vilatte's division, which had been directed to attack General Wilson at Numbella, had found no enemy there; that General Wilson had retired on the 4th; and that the inhabitants of Numbella stated his retreat to have been occasioned by the arrival of a corps of French troops at Placentia.[3]

Marshal the Duke of Belluno went on the 6th to Santa Olalla; from which place he acquainted your Majesty, that the Anglo-Spanish army had quitted Talavera on the 4th, proceeding towards Placentia: that the cavalry of the 1st corps would that day (the 6th) reach Talavera, and that General Wellesley had recommended to him 4000 wounded, whom he had been obliged to leave behind him in that town.

Marshal the Duke of Belluno advanced on the 7th to Talavera, with his whole corps of the army. The same day the cavalry of the 1st corps formed a junction at Oropesa, and at Puerte de l'Arzobispo, with the troops of the Duke of Dalmatia.

---

3. This was the first information that the enemy received of Soult's movements, so that the operations of the Legion prevented a junction between the French Army and Soult's corps until the 7th; and thus enabled the uninterrupted movements and subsequent retreat of the combined Anglo-Spanish Army over the Tagus.

Appendix, M

BATTLE OF BAINOS

Bulletin from the London Gazette of September 9, 1809

Downing Street, Sept. 7, 1809.
Dispatches, of which the following are copies and extracts, were this day received at the office of Viscount Castlereagh, one of His Majesty's Principal Secretaries of State, from Lieutenant-General Viscount Wellington, K. B.

Truxillo, Aug. 21, 1909.
My Lord,
When I marched from Talavera on the 3rd instant, with a view to oppose the French corps which we had heard had passed through the Puerte de Bainos, and had arrived at Placentia, Sir Robert Wilson was detached upon the left of the army, towards Escalona; and before I marched on that morning, I pat him in communication with the Spanish General Cuesta, who it had been settled was to remain at Talavera. I understood that General Cuesta put Sir Robert in communication with his advanced guard, which retired from Talavera on the night of the 4th.

Sir Robert Wilson, however, did not arrive at Valada till the night of the 4th, having made a long march through the mountains: and as he was then six leagues from the bridge of Arzobispo, and had to cross the high road from Oropesa to Talavera, of which the enemy was in possession, he conceived that he was too late to retire to Arzobispo, and he determined to move to Venta St. Julien and Catinello towards the Tietar, and across that river towards the mountains which separate Castille from Estremadura.

Some of Sir Robert Wilson's dispatches having missed me, I am not aware by which of the passes he went through the mountains, but I believe by Tornavacas.[1]

He arrived, however, at Bainos on the 11th, and on the 12th was attacked and defeated by the French corps of Marshal Ney, which, with that of Soult, returned to Placentia on the 9th, 10th, and 11th, that of Ney having since gone on towards Salamanca.

I enclose Sir Robert Wilson's account of the action. He as well as the other British officers of his corps, have been very active, intelligent, and useful in the command of the Portuguese and Spanish corps with which they were detached from this army.

Before the battle of the 28th of July, he had pushed his parties almost to the gates of Madrid, with which city he was in communication; and he would have been in Madrid, if I had not thought it proper to call him in, in expectation of that general action which took place on the 28th of July.

He afterwards alarmed the enemy on the right of his army; and throughout the service, shewed himself an active and intelligent partisan, well acquainted with the country in which he was acting, and possessing the confidence of the troops which he commanded.

Being persuaded that his retreat was not open by Arzobispo, he acted right in taking the road he did, with which he was well acquainted; and although unsuccessful in the action which he fought, (which may well be accounted for, by the superior numbers and description of the enemy's troops,) the action, in my opinion, does him great credit.

I have the honour to be,
&c. &c. &c.
(Signed)   Arthur Wellesley.

Miranda de Castenar, Aug. 13, 1809.

Sir,

I have the honour to acquaint you, that I was on march yesterday morning on the road of Grenadelia from Aldea Nueva, to restore my communication with the allied army, when a peas-

---

1. Sir Robert Wilson was obliged to re-cross the Tietar, to drive from Aldea Nueva a detachment of the enemy occupying that town, and to carry by storm, at night, the village of Viranda, strongly occupied by the enemy, and then to pass over the Sierra Liana, a ridge of mountains eternally covered with snow: from thence he proceeded to Bohoyo, Barco d'Avila, Bejar, and Bainos.

ant assured us, that a considerable quantity of dust, which we perceived in the road of Placentia, proceeded from the march of a body of the enemy.

I immediately returned and took post in front of Bainos, with my piquets in advance of Aldea Nueva, selecting such points for defence as the exigency of the time permitted.

The enemy's cavalry advanced on the high road, and drove back my small cavalry posts; but a piquet of Spanish infantry, which I had concealed, poured in on the cavalry a steady and well-directed fire, that killed and wounded many of them.

The two hundred Spanish infantry in advance of Aldea Nueva, continued, under the direction of Colonel Grant and their officers, to maintain their ground most gallantly, until the enemy's cavalry and *chasseurs à cheval*, in considerable bodies, appeared on both flanks, when they were obliged to retreat.

The enemy's *chasseurs à cheval* and cavalry advanced in great numbers in every direction, and pushed to cut off the Legion posted between Aldea Nueva and Bainos; but, by the steady conduct of officers and men, the enemy could only advance gradually, and with a very severe loss from the commanding fire thrown on them.

The Merida battalion, however, having given way on the right, a road was laid open, which cut behind our position, and I was obliged to order a retreat on the heights above Bainos, when I was again necessitated to detach a corps, in order to scour the road of Monte Major, by which I saw the enemy directing a column, and which road turned altogether the Puerte de Bainos, a league in our rear.

At this time Don Carlos Marquis de Espaine came up with his battalion of light infantry, and in a most gallant manner took post along the heights commanding the road of Bainos, which enabled me to send some of the Merida battalion on the mountain on our left, commanding the main road, and which the enemy had tried to ascend.

This battalion of light infantry, and the detachment of the Legion on its right, continued, notwithstanding the enemy's fire of artillery and musketry, to maintain their ground; but, at six o'clock in the evening, three columns of the enemy mounted the height on our left, gained it, and poured such a fire on the troops below, that longer defence was impracticable, and the whole was obliged to retire on the mountains on our left, leaving open the main road, along which a considerable column of cavalry immediately poured.

The battalion of Seville had been left at Bejar with orders to follow me next clay; but when I was obliged to return, and the action commenced, I ordered it to Puerte de Bainos, to watch the Monte Major road and the heights in the rear of our left.

When the enemy's cavalry came near, an officer and some dragoons called out to the commanding officer to surrender, but a volley killed him and his party, and then the battalion proceeded to mount the heights, in which movement it was attacked and surrounded by a column of cavalry and a column of infantry, but cut its way and cleared itself, killing a great many of the enemy, especially of his cavalry.

The enemy is now passing to Salamanca with great expedition. I lament that I could no longer arrest his progress; but, when the enormous superiority of the enemy's force is considered, and that we had no artillery, and that the Puerto de Bainos, on the Estremaduran side, is not a pass of such strength as on the side of Castille, especially without guns, I hope that a resistance for nine hours, which must have cost the enemy a great many men, will not be deemed inadequate to our means.

I have to acknowledge the services rendered me on this occasion by Colonel Grant, Major Human, Don Ferman Marquis. Adjutant-Major of the Dragoons of Pavia, Captain Charles and Mr. Bolman; and to express the greatest approbation of two companies of the Merida battalions advanced in front, and of the commanding officer and soldiery of the battalions of Seville, and the Portuguese brigades. I have already noticed the distinguished conduct of Don Carlos, and his battalion merits the highest encomiums.

I have not yet been able to collect the returns of our loss. From the nature of mountain warfare, many men are missing who cannot join for a day or two; but I believe the enemy will only have to boast that he has achieved his passage, and his killed and wounded will be a great diminution of his victory.

 I have the honour to be, &c.

Robert Wilson.

Sir A. Wellesley, &c., &c., &c.

Extracts from the *Moniteur*.

Marshal Soult to the Governor of Avila.

Wilson's corps is cut off, and cannot escape; if you send 1500 men to Candelabria, it must surrender.[2]

Report of the Duke of Elchingen to Marshal Soult.

On the 8th, while the army was taking the bridge of Arzobispo, I had detachments on the right bank of the Tietar, near Villa Nueva, to watch the corps of the English General Wilson.

On the 12th, the corps of the army set out *en masse*, from Placentia. On reaching Oliva, I learnt the enemy occupied in force Aldea Nueva, and principally the heights and defiles of Bainos. My advanced guard, under General Lorcet, composed of *voltigeurs* of the 25th Light Infantry, 2750; 59th regiment of the line, 23rd Dragoons, and 15th of Hussars, a battalion of light artillery, Colonel Armano's brigade of dragoons, &c. actually fell in With the enemy at Aldea Nueva. The attack and success were equally rapid. The position was taken, and the 3rd Hussars made an admirable charge.

The routed enemy rejoined, in small companies, his principal corps on the heights of Bainos. These were occupied by General Wilson with 4000 or 5000 men. That general, who considered his position impregnable, had added to the difficulties of ground, by obstructing the accessible paths with abattis, ditches, and masses of rock. As soon as the artillery of the army had closed at Bainos, they marched against the enemy, and forgot their fatigues. The 59th and 60th regiments advanced against the heights with great boldness, and made themselves masters of the heights, which were obstinately defended.

General Wilson, however, rallied his troops for the third time, and even endeavoured again to act on the offensive, hoping to overthrow us in his turn; but this attempt was extremely disastrous to himself. The advanced guard had united, and an engagement with the bayonet commenced, in which the enemy was overwhelmed.

The hussars and *chasseurs* assisted in putting him completely to the rout: in short, this little corps, which left 1200 in the field, is entirely destroyed. Our dragoons fought on foot on several oc-

---

2 The same notice was sent to Marshal Jourdan, Joseph Buonaparte, and other generals.

casions, and distinguished themselves. The artillery also behaved well. The loss that we have sustained in the late battles amounts to 5 officers and 30 subalterns and privates killed; 10 officers and 140 subalterns and privates wounded; several dropped dead in the ranks from heat and fatigue.

Monsieur Terrier L'Enque, Colonel of the 3rd Hussars, distinguished himself in several charges, and that regiment lost 40 horses. Colonel Cosel, of the 59th Infantry, killed an officer, who, while charging, attempted to take his horse.

Appendix, N

The Combined Army takes up a position on the right bank of the Mondego.

St. Martinho do Bispo, Sept. 30, 1810.

On the morning of the 3rd instant, the first division marched upon the road to Coimbra, five leagues. General Cameron's brigade and the 3rd Guards hutted; the Coldstream was quartered in Moita, and the King's German Legion in an adjoining village. Next day, the 3rd Guards marched to the village of Sanguinhada, and General Cameron's brigade, on the 5th, was cantoned in Cortica.

Headquarters were at Gouvea, and every thing remained quiet in front. The 24th Portuguese regiment, taken in Almeida, and said to have volunteered into the French service, has every man escaped.

At daybreak on the 18th instant, the Guards marched from Moita and Sanguinhada; at the same time, the rest of the division was in motion, and the whole crossed the Ponte de Marcella and bivouacked two leagues beyond, near the village of Foy d'Arouce, on the banks of the River Ceira. Thunder and lightning, with heavy rains, continued without intermission the whole of the night and following morning.

Before daybreak on the 19th, the division was again on march, and entered Coimbra soon after mid-day.

Headquarters were yesterday at Castica, and this morning Lord Wellington with his Staff, accompanied by Marshal Beresford, crossed the Mondego.

During the night, several Portuguese regiments came into Coimbra.

At half-past 9 a.m. on the 20th, the division advanced on the Oporto road, and halted at Malheada, in which town the 3rd Guards were quartered.

The Coldstream halted in a wood on the right. Colonel Pack-enham's brigade, the 7th and 79th, were in advance, Lord Blantyre (Cameron's) on the left, and the King's German Legion half a mile in the rear.

Sept. 21st, before dawn, the division was under arms. The 3rd Guards moved out of Malheada to join the Coldstream, when Colonel Packenham's brigade went into cantonments. Several brigades of Portuguese infantry formed in the rear of the division, on the Coimbra road.

Sept. 22nd, the Coldstream went into quarters at Valcaliza, and the 3rd regiment in the villages of Travassa and Canedo.

The fall of Almeida, after a bombardment of only one day, but in reality occasioned by the explosion of the grand magazine, by which unfortunate event one half of the town was destroyed, 500 of the garrison, and a great number of the inhabitants killed, removed the principal remaining obstacle to the entrance of Massena's army into this kingdom; but they proceeded with great caution in their movements, owing to the difficulty of bringing forward their supplies, which was absolutely necessary, as the enemy would not place any dependence on the resources of a country so long occupied by the British.

The French appear to have been completely foiled in their plans by the prudent defensive system adopted by Lord Wellington; as there can be no doubt that it was a principal object with Massena, in undertaking the sieges of Ciudad Rodrigo and Almeida, to draw the British from their strong hilly positions to the plains on which these towns are situated, where, if at all, the superior number of his cavalry might be expected to give him the advantage. On a further advance from the frontier, that species of force could no longer be rendered useful in the same degree, but must prove extremely burthensome and embarrassing to his operations, from the very great scarcity of forage, which even the British experienced at times, although the harvest had been got in, and the whole grain in the country was in requisition for their supply.

About a fortnight ago, Marshal Massena made a feint of coming down upon the left bank of the Mondego, and actually pushed his reconnoitring parties to Cortico and Linhares in that direction; but, apprehensive of meeting a check at the strong pass of the Ponte de Marcella, he, on the 18th, 19th, and 20th of September, crossed the river, with his whole army, at the bridge of Fornas, below Celerico, advancing upon Coimbra by the way of Vizeu. This movement of the enemy was met by the commander of the forces with his usual fore-sight; and the intentions of the French leader being now clearly de-veloped, the 2nd division, under General Hill, was directed to join the main body by the route of Sobriera Formosa, and Perdegao, when the whole of the combined army, with the exception of General Fane's division of cavalry and some Portuguese infantry, was placed upon the right bank of the Mondego, with a celerity which set all ordinary calculation at defiance.

Sept. 22nd, skirmishing at the outposts.

On the 23rd, the bridge over the Criz, beyond Mortigao, hav-ing been blown up by Brigadier-General Pack, the French occupied themselves in repairing it, and then passed over a column of infan-try and cavalry, who were opposed by the light division and General Pack's Portuguese brigade.

On the 24th and 25th, the enemy continued to advance, and it was evident the whole of his force was concentrating. In a smart skirmish, Captain Hoey was severely, and Mellish slightly wounded.

Whilst the French continued their approach upon Coimbra, by the road leading over the Sierra of Busaco, the main body of the al-lied army remained in the adjoining villages, where the troops had been cantoned, that they might not suffer from the heavy dews at this season of the year.

Before daybreak on the 26th, the several divisions of British and Portuguese were in motion. The brigade of Guards arrived in the vil-lage of Luz about 8 o'clock, and soon after began to ascend the Sierra of Busaco, on whose summit is situated a convent of the austere order of La Trappe, which was Lord Wellington's headquarters. The route lay for nearly two miles through the gardens; before leaving them a cannonade commenced, the brigade was ordered to load, and then formed behind the brow of the hill, from whence the whole of the enemy's force was distinctly discerned. They appeared in considerable numbers; the infantry supposed to be not less than 10,000, and a very large force in cavalry.

About 5 p. m. the French piquets made an attack upon the Portu-guese light troops (*Caçadores*), who returned their fire with the utmost steadiness and resolution.

THE FORMATION OF THE COMBINED ARMY AS FOLLOWS:

Lieutenant-General Hill's division, which had crossed the Mon-dego this morning, was placed on the right of the whole line, having the divisions of Generals Leith and Picton on his left. In the centre, was the 1st division, of which the Guards formed the right, under the command of Sir Brent Spencer: beyond was the light division, in the most advanced part of the position, opposite the gardens of the monastery. Major-General Cole's at the extremity on the left.

General Fane's division of cavalry remained on the left bank of the Mondego, to observe the movements of the enemy in that direction; a few squadrons only were on the heights, the ground being unfavourable for that description of force; and the main body, under Sir Stapleton Cotton, was formed in the plains in the front of Malheada, and on the Oporto road.

The brigades of Portuguese infantry and *Caçadores* were united with the British, and the result proved this to have been the best possible distribution, of the troops of our ally.

The line of the combined army thus posted, extended along the ridge of Busaco for nearly two leagues; but the whole of the intermediate space was not occupied, except by a chain of light troops, and formed the segment of a circle, whose extreme points embraced every part of the enemy's position. Not a movement could be made in the French lines without its being immediately observed from the Sierra, and this circumstance contributed most materially to the success of the British.

At dusk, the 1st division moved to the right, and bivouacked close to the brow of the hill, covered by the light infantry. The weather thick and foggy.

Sept. 27th, at dawn of day, the enemy advanced in two columns, and at the same moment threatened the right and centre of the allied army. The column on the right moved up the hill, under the fire of the light troops, with great intrepidity, and had gained the summit when it was charged, whilst deploying into line, in the most gallant manner, by Colonel Mackinnon's[1] brigade, the 45th and 88th regiments, and the 9th Portuguese under Lieut. Col. Sutton, supported on the right by part of General Leith's corps, and on the left by Major-General Lightburne's brigade and the Guards, which had moved to the right for that purpose, on the first indication of the enemy's intention.

The French could not withstand the shock, but retreated down the hill with immense loss. One regiment, the 1st Legère of Regnier's Corps d'Armée, was entirely cut to pieces. The enemy, foiled in this

1. Colonel Mackinnon was killed at the head of his brigade (then a Major-General) by the blowing up of a mine at the capture of Ciudad Roderigo.

attack, made another more to the right, where he was again repulsed at the point of the bayonet. This second attack was supported by some heavy artillery, and dismounted two guns; but a shell having set fire to the ammunition-tumbril, which blew up, the French abandoned their battery.

The commander of the forces was every where in person, giving directions and superintending the different points of attack. Lieutenant-Colonel Campbell and Lord Fitzroy Somerset were wounded.

Finding these attacks on the right unsuccessful, the enemy directed his principal efforts against the left centre; and, in a charge made by the 43rd and 52nd regiments, General Simon was wounded and taken with his *aide-de-camp*. A short time afterwards, a young Spanish lady in male attire, whom the general had carried off from Madrid, with his baggage, was sent to the British headquarters with a flag of truce.

About 8 o'clock a fog came on, which, for a time, partially obscured the positions of the respective armies. When the day cleared up, it was discovered that the enemy had placed large bodies of light troops in the woods and valley which skirted the bottom of the Sierra, They were successfully opposed by the light division, the *Caçadores*, the light infantry of the 1st division, and Colonel Pakenham's brigade, the 7th and 79th regiments. The enemy's fire slackened about noon, but the light troops continued engaged until the evening. During the action, a number of deserters came over.

On the following morning, the light infantry were again partially engaged on the left of the line. At mid-day the enemy's cavalry, and several columns of infantry, were observed in motion to the rear. All quiet in camp. The French set fire to a small village on leaving it.

At 10 p.m. the army quitted the position of Busaco. After halting for two hours near the monastery, the 1st division proceeded on the road to Coimbra. At daylight on the 29th, it was perceived that the enemy had withdrawn the whole of his troops from the ground he occupied during the engagement.

An hour before sunset the division halted within a league of Coimbra, and this morning the troops were again under arms before daybreak. About 8 o'clock the Guards, in the rear of the column, forded the Mondego, and went into quarters in the village of St. Martinho do Bispo. Strong piquets were formed to protect the fords during the night.

Appendix, O

Portella de Casaes, 10th Nov. 1810.

The manoeuvres of Marshal Massena after the Battle of Busaco, left the commander of the forces in no doubt of his intention to throw his whole army on the high road from Oporto, and the position being turned on the 29th of September, by the enemy's movement to the right, Lord Wellington, in pursuance of the defensive system, on which he had hitherto acted, commenced his retreat to the fortified lines in the neighbourhood of the capital.

On the 1st of October, Sir Brent Spencer's division moved out of their cantonments before day break, and passing through the town of Pereira and Souré, bivouacked at dusk in a vineyard close to the latter,

The roads were crowded with people flying from their houses to the mountains and sea coast; the monasteries and nunneries were deserted; numbers accompanied the march of the British troops, and the banks of the Mondego were lined with distressed groups, impatiently waiting to embark.

The advance of the enemy on this morning entered Coimbra, their cavalry having previously charged a troop of horse artillery, which retired without loss over the Mondego.

October the 2nd, after a fatiguing march of five leagues, on a road parallel with the one through Pombal, by which the main body of the army was retiring, the 1st division halted on the banks of the Rio Maganche, within a league of Leyria, through which the troops marched next morning, and bivouacked in a wood, a league and a half beyond, near Canveiza, until the 5th, when the columns were again in motion, and halted at the close of day, near the village of Condexas.

On the 6th, the army marched through Rio Mayor to Alcoentre, four leagues, and on the 7th, to Aldea Gallega, the same distance, and bivouacked each day.

Heavy rains set in on the following morning, and the roads were in a dreadful state.

The 1st division passed through Sobral about noon, and the battalions were cantoned in the adjoining villages.

The Guards were at San Quintino, within a short distance of the works.

The cavalry under Sir Stapleton Cotton covered the retreat of the army, during the whole of the march from Busaco, and on several occasions, particularly at Leyria, on the 5th instant, proved its decided superiority over that of the enemy.

October the 9th, heavy rains. The troops remained in their quarters. The state of the roads necessarily retarded the enemy's advance to the position.

October the 10th, the whole division were in Sobral. The commander of the forces, and Marshal Beresford, arrived at San Quintino.

Next day the troops marched from Sobral, at two in the afternoon, and remained until dusk on the brow of a hill, in front of the grand batteries. Afterwards the Guards moved into the village of Sobriera. Heavy rains, with thunder and lightning; but the enemy continued to advance, notwithstanding the severity of the weather.

October the 12th, all quiet. The troops were kept in readiness to turn out at a moment's notice.

On the 13th. a strong column of the enemy was observed on the height, beyond Sobral, apparently moving towards the left. The gunboats, under the command of Lieutenant Berkeley, stationed in the Tagus, abreast of Villa Franca, opened a heavy fire this morning upon the town, in which there was a French force of 1200 men. who were driven out with considerable loss. General Lacroix was cut in two by a cannon shot.

Working parties were employed in completing the works on Sobriera Hill, and in mending the road to [1] Bucellas. The high road to Mafia runs through this village. All quiet during the night.

About noon on the 14th, the enemy opened a battery of four pounders, from behind some casks, at the entrance of Sobral, upon

1. The wine of that name is produced here.

the advance of the 1st division, consisting of the 71st regiment, under Colonel Cadogan, and part of Major-General Cameron's brigade. After a severe conflict of an hour, the enemy's fire was discontinued, and each party carried off their wounded. In this affair the French lost 100 men, British 40, in killed and wounded. A few prisoners were taken, but no advantage gained on either side. The piquets remained at dusk within a short distance of Sobral, which was occupied by the enemy, whose force being increased towards the evening, by the arrival of the 8th corps, and part of the 6th, Sir Brent Spencer, in the course of the night, withdrew his advanced posts.

At daybreak the next morning, a reconnoitring party of the enemy was observed on the heights where Major-General Cameron's brigade was posted the day before. About 7 a. m. the light infantry of the Guards moved out of Cabedos, in which a company of the 60th was left. Several working parties employed in mining the roads for explosion. The report of Colonel Trant having taken 5000 of the enemy's sick and wounded in Coimbra, now reached the French Army, and created a considerable sensation among the troops, whom the officers endeavoured to persuade that the news was unfounded.

Massena, attended by a large staff, was distinctly seen reconnoitring for a considerable, time. His army was in three divisions, and the right did not appear to be advanced beyond Sobral, his left extended to the Tagus. The road to Torres Vedras was rendered nearly impassable by the rains, which continued almost as violent as during the last week. It was now discovered by the French that they were in a very awkward predicament, in consequence of their rapid advance. Massena met with an opposition he certainly did not expect, and his difficulties hourly increased, from the want of provisions.

At 5 p. m. the Guards moved out of Sobriera to Portella de Casaes, to make room for Major-General Sir W. Erskine's brigade.

THE FOLLOWING WAS THE DISPOSITION OF THE COMBINED ARMY.

2nd Division—Gen. Hill's—the right resting at Alhandra, on the Tagus, and flanked by gunboats. The brigades of Generals Lumley and Hoghton, at Bucellas.

Light div.—Gen. Crawford's, under canvas.

5th *ditto*,—Gen. Leith's *ditto*

1st Division—Sir B. Spencer, centre and left. The general's headquarters in Sobriera.

3rd Division—Gen. Picton's, Torres Vedras.

4th Division—Gen. Cole's, Dias Portas.

6th Division—Gen. A. Campbell's, Ribaldiera.

Cavalry—Headquarters of Sir S. Cotton, at Mafra.

The Portuguese brigades in the batteries, and intermixed with the British. Brigadier-General Pack commanded in the fort, on the most elevated point, and in the centre of the entrenched line. From this spot, which is immediately above the village of Portella de Casaes, there is a most beautiful and extensive view; comprehending on the right, the rich valley of the Tagus, and across that river into the province of Alentejo, and on the left, to the Atlantic, including the whole of the positions, the hill of Cintra, and the Burlings, with the fortress of Peniché.

October 16th, all quiet. The sick sent daily to Lisbon. Working parties employed on the works, and in repairing some roads, and blocking up others. All communications to the commander of the forces were sent by the telegraphs on the hills, under the command of naval officers, and signals for the several brigades to march to their respective alarm posts, directed to be made on the first appearance of a forward movement by the enemy.

On the 19th, the Marquis of Romana crossed the Tagus below Villa Franca, with the 1st division of the Spanish army, under General O'Donnell.

The principal part of the French infantry were halted in a pine wood, about a league in rear of Sobral, which they continued to occupy. The enemy had no troops to the right of that town, therefore it was supposed that the attack, when made with a view of penetrating to Lisbon, would be either by the high road, leading from Sobral to that city, or by the road on the bank of the Tagus, which, in addition to the troops and batteries in that part of the line, was flanked by the gunboats, and Lieutenant Berkeley, who had already driven him out of Villa Franca. Massena at no time seemed to have entertained the idea of forcing his way to the capital, by the road on the sea side, from Torres Vedras through Mafra and Cintra.

October 28, the heavy rains were succeeded for the last week by fine dry healthy weather; the mornings cold. Deserters continued to arrive, who affirmed that the enemy's baggage was sent to the rear, and that a considerable force under Loison, had already fallen back upon Thomar, doubtless with a view of collecting provisions, of which (particularly bread) the troops were in great want.

Brigadier-General Blunt sent out parties from Peniché, who were constantly harassing the enemy's right: several skirmishes took place near Obidos, where there was a small Portuguese garrison, commanded by Captain Fenwick.

Major-General Fane now crossed the Tagus with a division of cavalry and infantry, to prevent the enemy foraging in the Alentejo.

Appendix, P

Retreat of Massena from Santarem, and advance of the British operations during the pursuit, which are continued until the whole of the Army of Portugal cross the Agueda, leaving Almeida to its fate— French barbarity.

Almadilla, Spain, 15th April, 1811.

Intelligence having reached the British headquarters in the beginning of March, that the enemy had been for some days employed in sending his heavy artillery and baggage, with the sick, to the rear, it became evident that the French commander-in-chief had some important movement in contemplation, On the 4th a large convent in Santarem was perceived on fire; at dusk on the following day the enemy withdrew his piquets, and the whole of the remaining force evacuated the town about midnight.

On the morning of the 5th of March General Picton's division moved forward, the enemy having withdrawn his troops from the vicinity of Rio Mayor.

Soon after daybreak on the 6th, the light division entered Santarem, and, in the course of that day, the 1st, 4th, and 6th divisions of infantry arrived in the town. The enemy, during his stay, had omitted no means of improving his position, which, in consequence, was found remarkably strong. It appears that there were never more than five or six regiments in Santarem, and those very sickly, which agrees with the accounts uniformly received from prisoners and deserters.

The light division arrived about noon at Pernis, which the rear guard of the French quitted before daylight, having effectually destroyed the two arches of the bridge. These, however, were speedily repaired by the staff corps for the passage of infantry.

On the 7th the troops were under arms at an early hour, when the Guards and King's German Legion marched to Pernis, the 4th and 6th divisions to Golegao. Headquarters on this day at Torres Novas.

Pernis, where Junot had been stationed for some weeks, is situated in a fertile valley, watered by the Aveila in its course to the Tagus.

About 200 yards above the bridge the river, tumbling over broken rocks, forms a grand and romantic cascade; the banks being extremely confined and fringed with wood, through which the stream is seen rushing, add to the beauty of the surrounding objects: a ruined mill, covered with ivy, and some old houses overhanging the river, contiguous to the fall, contribute further to enrich the scenery, which is in the highest degree picturesque. Under a projection of the cliff lay the mutilated remains of a Frenchman, who, having straggled from his party, had been put to death by the peasantry.

There were few inhabitants in Pernis, and these in great distress for want of subsistence, the French having; on their arrival seized on every article of provision for their own use, regardless of the misery this occasioned to the wretched Portuguese.

On the 8th, the artillery of the 1st division crossed the river at the ford a little below the bridge, and were parked on the opposite heights; the troops remained in their quarters, ready to move at a moment's notice.

On the 9th, the main body of the French under Massena took the Coimbra road. General Regnier, with the 2nd corps, marched towards Espinhel, and Loison's division by Anciao.

About ten o'clock the Guards and King's German Legion marched from Pernis, and at 3 p. m. reached Torres Novas, for some time Massena's headquarters.

At five the brigade was again in motion, and in four hours the 3rd regiment halted in the village of Slides, where there were few inhabitants. Roads very bad; the guns in consequence took a circuitous route to the right through Atalaya.

On the 10th, the brigade advanced to Pyalvo, where the Coldstream regiment had been cantoned the preceding night. The brigade then proceeded on march, and about noon came up with the rear of the 4th division, on the road from Thomar to Leyria. General Cole had been ordered across the Tagus to reinforce Marshal Beresford, but was recalled on Massena's movement being distinctly ascertained. In the afternoon heavy showers of rain. About 4 p. m. halted near the miserable village of Cachairas. Colonel De Grey's brigade of cavalry, the King's German Legion, and 4th division on the same ground. The whole of the troops in bivouac. Before dusk Major-General Hoghton's corps from the 2nd division reached the camp.

At daybreak on the 11th of March, the troops were in motion, and proceeded left in front on the road to Pombal; the 6th division joined the column, the head of which, after a long and fatiguing march, arrived near the town at dusk. Pombal had been set on fire by the enemy, who failed in his attempt to hold the ancient castle, and was driven out by the light division. About 9 p. m. the enemy's fires in front of the town were observed going out; but a considerable force remained in bivouac, at the distance of a league.

The whole of the army was collected near Pombal in the course of this evening.

Next morning (the 12th,) the British columns advanced along the road to Condeixa, part of the troops fording the river, while the rest moved over the bridge, and through the town, in pursuit of the enemy, whose rear-guard, commanded this day by Marshal Ney, was brought to action in front of the village of Redinha, their right on the Souré River screened by a wood; from whence, after a gallant stand, they were dislodged by Sir Brent Spencer, with the 3rd, 4th, and light divisions, and the troops following the enemy briskly across the narrow bridge over the Redinha River drove him upon the main body at Condeixa. During this operation the remaining divisions were in reserve. The army bivouacked for the night close to Redinha. The 6th division under General A. Campbell made a lateral movement this morning upon the enemy s right by way of Souré.

On the 13th, the allied army was again in motion at day-break. The main body, with the artillery, marched upon the high road, while General Picton advanced along the heights on the right, with some mountain guns. Soon after mid-day the columns closed up and bivouacked within a league of Condeixa, which was observed on lire. The light division was, for a short time, partially engaged with the enemy's rear.

March the 14th, the troops moved off their ground about 7 o'clock, and advanced towards Condeixa. In several places the enemy had constructed abattis to retard the pursuit: these obstacles, however, were soon overcome, and the columns, with the exception of Major-General Picton's division, which moved along the heights and manoeuvred upon the enemy's left, passed through the once beautiful, but now ruined town of Condeixa. Meanwhile, the light division, supported by the 6th, was warmly engaged with the enemy, whose sharp-shooters, advantageously posted behind stone walls, took a deliberate aim upon the advance of the British.

This irregular warfare continued for some hours, after which the enemy retired to a hill, one league in front of Miranda de Corvo, in consequence of the movements made on his flanks by General Picton, and the light division under Sir William Erskine. From a height on which the light division bivouacked, the French were observed in considerable force. Regnier, who had taken the Espinhel road, followed by Major-General Nightingale, effected a junction this day with the main body under the Prince of Esling, whose whole army was now assembled in one solid mass.

In the course of the morning several officers were wounded: Major Stewart of the 95th, Captain Napier of the 43rd, and Captain George T. Napier of the 52nd. Major Napier of the 50th, who had been severely wounded in the Battle of Corunna, was sent for to his brother's, when a most affecting scene took place.

March the 15th. The morning was extremely foggy, which proved favourable to the enemy, whose movements were thereby concealed. About 9 the day cleared up, previous to which, the light division under Sir William Erskine, the 3rd (Picton's,) and 6th (A. Campbell's,) advanced in pursuit. Some deserters came in, who said that the French were destroying their artillery and burning a quantity of ammunition. At 11, the 1st division marched, and about 3 p. m. passed through the smoking ruins of Miranda de Corvo. The roads throughout were strewed with animals, destroyed carriages and baggage, and numbers of dead and wounded Frenchmen. At 5, the light division and Major-General Picton's, supported by the 1st and 6th divisions, and two brigades of cavalry, brought the enemy's rear to action near the village of Foy d'Arouce. The firing continued until dusk, when the French retreated in confusion, and with considerable loss across the Ceira River, in which many were drowned.

On the 16th of March, at 4 a. m. the enemy blew up the bridge over the Ceira, keeping a force on the opposite bank to watch the fords. This day the army halted for supplies, which there was found some difficulty in bringing forward; the roads at all times bad, having been much cut up by the late heavy rains. General Cole and Colonel de Grey proceeded to join Marshal Beresford in the Alentejo.

On the 17th March, the enemy's rear-guard moved off during the night, and at day-break the advance of the British forded the river near the bridge. Soon after the 1st division crossed at a ford, about a mile above, upon which the enemy had brought two guns to bear on the preceding day.

On the 18th March the army advanced towards the Ponte de Marcella, over which the whole of the enemy had now retired and destroyed the bridge, leaving a strong corps to observe the ford. About 2 p. m. the 1st division halted near the village of Pombeiro, where Lord Wellington fixed his headquarters. The enemy was posted in force on the right bank of the Alva. During the whole of this retreat, the French made their marches by night, putting their troops in motion a few hours after dusk.

The 19th March. This morning thick and foggy, in consequence the troops remained in their huts until noon, when the fog dispersed. The 3rd division marched to Arganil; about 5, the Guards at the head of the 1st division arrived on the bank of the Alva, which they forded mid-deep: night coming on, the 5th division halted on the left bank. There was some difficulty in getting the artillery across.

A number of prisoners were made on this day, having been sent out for the purpose of collecting provisions in the neighbouring villages; and from this circumstance, it is believed to have been Massena's intention to have halted on the right bank of the Alva to refresh his army, had he not found himself so closely pursued. The troops bivouacked in the position of Moita, where they remained waiting for their supplies until noon on the 25th, when the column proceeded on the road to Celerico. At dusk the 1st division halted near the village of Galizes. The 5th division, Major-General Dunlop's, in the rear, within a short distance.

At daybreak on the 26th, the British advanced four leagues, and about dusk our brigade went into quarters at St. Martinho and St. Marinha; Major-General Howard's at St. Romao: General Nightingall's at Cea, and the King's German Legion at Penhancos. The artillery at the Quinta de Beca. which, with the palace at Cea, had been burnt to the ground. Headquarters in Gouvea: 3rd division. General Picton's, at Linhares.

The advance at Celerico, in which the enemy had destroyed a few houses.

On the 27th, the army halted.

On the 28th, the 1st division advanced towards Celerico. and was cantoned this day in Mello; General Howard's in Sampayo, the King's German Legion in Gouvea, General Nightingall's in Villa Cortex and

Cortico. Headquarters in Celerico. Massena occupied Guarda with a considerable force; indeed the numbers of the retreating army are computed at nearly 50,000.

On the 29th, the 1st division marched to Celerico, and about sunset the troops were quartered in the town and the neighbouring villages of Chesu, Lagiosa, Val de Sierras, Frontilhera, &c. The artillery at Baracal. The principal arch of the bridge over the Mondego had been destroyed, but was now repaired for the passage of the allied army.

Massena left Guarda this morning with one corps of his army and part of another, on the appearance of the British columns. General Picton, with the 3rd division, moved across the Sierra d'Estrella, upon the enemy's left, by the mountain track from Monteigas; the light division advanced upon the right from Fraxedas, while General Alexander Campbell marched upon the high road through the valley of Mondego, and ascended the hill of Guarda in front of the city. This movement was so skilfully combined, that the heads of the several columns made their appearance on the heights of Guarda nearly at the same moment, and the celerity and precision of their manoeuvres so intimidated the enemy, that without firing a gun he immediately commenced his retreat towards the Coa, in the direction of Sabugal, pursued by the cavalry and light troops, who skirmished with the rear-guard and made about 300 prisoners.

As the French retired, the peasantry came with their implements of husbandry from their hiding places, and commenced their labours; in many places the vines were already trimmed, and the industrious farmer, busied in his fields, seemed anxious to repair the loss of time, and the devastation committed by the enemy.

March 30th, the division halted. On the following morning, the Guards marched five leagues to Fraxedas; the artillery and the King's German Legion halted in Alverca, which, during , the sieges of Ciudad Rodrigo and Almeida, had been Lord Wellington's headquarters; the route was through Celerico and Baracal.

April the 1st, the troops remained in their cantonments. At Fraxedas the enemy, in addition to their usual atrocities, violated the repose of the dead, by opening the graves in the church, which was in ruins, in hopes of finding valuables buried in the coffins, as they had done at Alcantara.

April 2. The army advanced towards the Coa, and the brigades of the 1st division were cantoned at nightfall in villages about a league from the river.

April 3. Soon after daybreak the army moved forward to attack the enemy in Sabugal, where General Regnier remained with the 2nd *corps d'armée.* About mid-day the action commenced by a brisk cannonade, and the enemy, being compelled to evacuate the town, drew up on an adjoining height, from whence they were dislodged by the light division in a most gallant manner before the other troops could come into action. General Picton advanced two miles in front of the town to the ground on which part of the enemy bivouacked. The attack being entirely unexpected, their tents were left standing, and were taken possession of with a considerable quantity of baggage, the greater part of which fell into the hands of the light division, whose conduct on this day obtained the approbation and thanks of Lord Wellington, and the admiration of the whole army.

The light division was quartered this evening in Sabugal, and the principal part of the army got under cover in the adjoining villages, although some of the troops were necessarily obliged to bivouac. Heavy rain during the greater part of the day. Headquarters at the Quinta of Gonsalvo Martinez in the vale of Monrisco, from whence they moved, next day, into Sabugal. The Guards were cantoned in the ruined village of St. Antonio, where they remained until the morning of the 5th, when the whole of the troops were again in motion. The Guards and Major-General Howard's brigade forded the Coa a mile and a half above Sabugal. This little town, which is on the Spanish side of the river, is of great antiquity, and surrounded with a wall. The handsome Moorish tower is still in great preservation.

At noon, the 7th division passed through the column, which then proceeded to Navé, in which town the Guards and Major-General Howard's brigade halted for the night.

April 6. The troops were in motion soon after daylight. The Guards, about 9 o'clock, passed through the ancient Moorish town of Alfayates, and two hours afterwards, reached Aldea Velha on the road to Villa Major. On the following day to Turcalhos, one league, and the whole of the British army now entered Spain again,

April 8. The 1st division halted, and, on the 9th, advanced over the frontier through Albegaria to the little village of Almadilla, two leagues from Villa Formosa, the headquarters. The light division, at the same time, moved forward to the 3rd instant at Sabugal, were on the point of firing a *feu-de-joie* in honour of the birth of the King of

Rome, the account of which had just been received from Paris.

After the action, Regnier made a forced march of 18 hours, and, on the 4th, reached the Agueda, over which the whole of the army, (destined for the subjugation of Portugal, and to drive the English into the sea) were very happy to retire.

The result of the operations in which the British Army had been engaged for the last five weeks was highly satisfactory; not a Frenchman at this moment remaining in the kingdom, with the exception of the garrison of Almeida, and the communication between this fortress and Ciudad Rodrigo was completely cut off; the combined army now occupied a line, the left of which was upon the Douro. The mode of warfare to which Lord Wellington restricted himself in this pursuit of Massena, proved extremely embarrassing to the troops of the enemy, while the British Army, having sustained few privations and undergone no unnecessary fatigue, was in the highest health and spirits, unbroken, and ready to enter upon any further operations to which they might be called. Massena's army, on the contrary, was known to be disorganised and dispirited, and for some weeks was not again in a condition to take the field.

The accounts constantly received, of the distress which the French suffered in the position at Santarem from a scarcity of provisions, and the consequent sickness of the troops, proved to be no exaggeration, and was fully confirmed by the inhabitants of these places occupied by the enemy, who, from a variety of causes, had remained in their homes. The French leader, apprehensive of being attacked on the arrival of the expected reinforcements from England, and fearing the consequences in the exhausted state of his army, at length determined upon a retreat, which was, in fact, become a matter of imperious necessity. However formidable the position at Santarem, the invincible spirit and superior discipline of British troops must have insured them complete success whenever an attack was determined upon. The French Army, for the purpose of foraging, occupied an extended line of country; and the force in the town was by no means adequate to maintain it had a division of troops passed the Tagus in its rear, whilst the attention of the enemy was directed to points more immediately threatened, by which the principal part of the attacking columns, owing to local circumstances, must, of necessity, have approached.

These considerations, and the distress of his army, had, doubtless, their weight on the mind of the French leader, who found himself in a situation of unexampled difficulty, to him, "the spoiled child of victory," altogether new, and to extricate from which, required the exertions of all his talents and of all his firmness. The reverse which the Prince of Essling experienced in his attempts to subjugate Portugal, must have been the more painful to his feelings, when he reflected, that he had for ever tarnished his military fame by his vain, arrogant, and premature boast in the face of the whole world, to drive the English into the sea, and plant the eagles of Napoleon on the towers of Lisbon.

To the last moment was the farce kept up, and his deluded troops endeavoured to forget their wants in hopes of the plunder of the metropolis, the sole object of their thoughts, for which they had made so many painful marches, and undergone the most severe privations. In the theatre at Santarem, which the French officers had fitted up for their amusement, the piece represented on the eve of this memorable retreat, and brought out with every adventitious aid of scenery, calculated to dazzle the senses and inflame the passions of the soldiery, was the "Frenchman in Lisbon!"

The most barbarous excesses were committed by the enemy throughout his whole line of march, and the inhabitants who, from age or sickness, were unable to quit their houses, became victims to the horrid brutality of the French soldiery. There is no atrocity of which these unprincipled ruffians have not been guilty; every crime that stains the black catalogue of human cruelty having been committed on the persons and property of the poor wretches who had the misfortune to fall into their hands. The prospect before the advanced guard was always that of burning villages; of plundered cottages; of murdered peasants.

The roads were covered with the dying and the dead; with cannon, baggage, and ammunition, which the enemy could not carry off; with mutilated cattle; with everything, in short, that could create horror and disgust—that could make the heart feel sentiments of indignation against the barbarous enemy, and of pity for the suffering and ravaged natives. Not infrequently, however, the latter were able to revenge upon the invader the cruelties he had committed. In some of the villages the peasants had cut off detachments of the enemy, and put them to instant death.

Nearly the whole of the once beautiful city of Leyria is reduced to ashes. The mansion of the rich, and the cottage of the poor, were alike the objects of the enemy's vengeance, and involved in one common conflagration by the merciless destroyer.

The magnificent convent of Alcobaca has been burnt by Massena's order, and Batalha would have shared the same fate but for the massive strength of its walls, which resisted the sacrilegious attempt.

A strong detachment of the *corps d'armée* which daily formed the rearguard of the retreating enemy, was specially allotted to carry the work of destruction into execution.

Appendix, Q

BATTLE OF FUENTES DE HONOR.

*Massena having collected the whole of the troops in the North of Spain,
makes an attempt to relieve Almeida.—Battle of Fuentes de Honor.—
Almeida abandoned by the garrison.*

Almadilla, 12th May, 1811.

Lord Wellington having learnt that the Prince of Essling had assembled a council of war at Ciudad Rodrigo on the 1st instant, which
was attended by twenty-six generals, and the enemy having for some
days previously made frequent demonstrations on the left bank of the
Agueda, it was supposed that the French chief meditated an attempt
to relieve Almeida, or, failing in that, to bring off the garrison, which
was known to be now in much distress for provisions.

On the following day the enemy crossed the river in force, and
drove the light division out of Gallegos. The whole of the troops, in
consequence, moved from their cantonments, and, on the 3rd, this part
of the army, under the immediate command of Lord Wellington, was
concentrated betwixt the villages of Fuentes de Honor in Spain, and
Villa Fermosa in Portugal, two leagues from Almeida, and four from
Ciudad Rodrigo.

In the course of the same day the French army, commanded by
Massena, having under him Marshals Marmont and Bessieres, and
General Loison, arrived on the plains on the other side of Fuentes, the
key of the British position, and, about two in the afternoon, pushed
forward several corps of sharpshooters to attack the village, which
was defended with the greatest obstinacy by the light troops; but the
enemy, from his superiority of numbers, at length obtained possession
of this important post, from which, however, he was soon after dislodged by the 71st Regiment, under Colonel Cadogan, at the point

175

of the bayonet. This was a little before dusk. Next morning the enemy renewed his attacks upon the village, but every effort proved unsuccessful.

At daybreak, on the 5th, it was perceived that the enemy had moved the whole of his cavalry, and several heavy columns of infantry, towards the right. About 6 o'clock his manoeuvres seemed to indicate an attack on that point, and, soon after, the cavalry, deriving confidence from their numbers, advanced upon the British, which was their weak arm, and compelled them to give way; but, in retreating, the British cavalry repeatedly faced about and made some successful charges upon the enemy. Meanwhile, the 7th division, which had been considerably advanced upon the plain, was directed to fall back and form on the brigade of Guards posted on the right of the 1st division, and flanked by Captain Lawson's brigade of 9-pounders, and some squadrons of cavalry.

Their *point d'appui* rested on some broken and rocky ground, intersected with enclosures of stone walls, and copse wood, having a small river, the Turon, in the rear.

Major-General Houston was enabled to execute this retrograde movement in the face of an infinitely superior force, principally by the steadiness and gallant conduct of the two foreign corps in his division, the Duke of Brunswick *Oels'* infantry, and the *Chasseurs Brittanniques*, under Lieutenant Colonel Eustace, who checked the advance of the French cavalry by several well directed volleys. The enemy had, previous to this, opened a tremendous fire upon the first line of infantry; every shot that went over doing execution in the second line.

The light division, which at first formed on the left of the 7th division, also retired before the enemy's cavalry in echelon of squares, and in the finest order.

About 11 a.m. the piquet of the Guards, consisting of 100 rank and file, under Lieutenant-Colonel Hill, skirmishing in front of the brigade, was charged by a squadron of cavalry, which they repulsed, and were retiring upon the 42nd Regiment, commanded by Lord Blantyre, formed in columns for the support of the light troops upon some broken ground, when the enemy returned to the attack in such numbers that, after seeing most of his officers and men cut down, Colonel Hill, being wounded, was compelled to surrender himself prisoner.

Ensign Cookson was killed; Ensign Stothert, of the Coldstream, wounded slightly and taken prisoner. Captains Home and Harvey escaped, although for some minutes in the enemy's hands, the latter slightly wounded. At this moment the 9-pounders having opened upon the French cavalry, they retired in great confusion. About the same time, the enemy pushed forward his light infantry upon the right, where they were met and repulsed by Colonel Guise, with the light companies of the guards, and part of the 95th Regiment, under Captain O'Hare.

The line was now formed with the 7th division on the right of the first division, having on its left General Crawford with the light division in reserve. Beyond were, those of Major-Generals Picton, A. Campbell, and Sir William Erskine. The left of the whole was on Fort Conception, covering Almeida.

The principal part of the cavalry remained on the right. Brigadier-General Pack was stationed with the Queen's Regiment and a brigade of Portuguese infantry watching Almeida, from whence guns were fired at intervals as signals.

The 7th division subsequently crossed the Turon, and formed upon the hill in rear of the present line, on which, should Lord Wellington think proper to refuse his right, a new position was intended to be taken up.

The firing slackened on both sides towards the evening, but the engagement was not finally over until the close of day, when the enemy, who was repulsed at all points, remained in the same position as at the commencement of the action, being unable to gain a single advantage or make the smallest impression upon any part of the British line.

The French Army is stated to have been not less than 40,000 infantry and 5000 cavalry when they entered the field. Their loss is estimated at from 1500 to 2,000 killed; and it is known that 3,500 wounded have been carried into Ciudad Rodrigo. Our loss has also been severe, amounting to 1,760 killed, wounded, and missing; but this number falls short of what might have been expected from the length of time the troops were under fire.

The principal contest was in Fuentes, the possession of which was of the utmost importance to either army. Colonel Cameron[1] was mortally wounded at the head of the 79th Regiment in defending this village.

The hostile armies remained in front of each other on the two

1. He was the eldest son of the gallant General Cameron, Colonel of the 79th Regiment. Another of his sons was killed in these campaigns.

following days, and, in the afternoon of the 7th, were employed in burying their dead.

During this interval working parties were constantly occupied in strengthening the position of the British by throwing up field-works.

The enemy having received a reinforcement, a renewal of the attack was generally expected on the morning of the 8th, instead of which, at daybreak, his cavalry videttes galloped off to the rear, and, soon after, several columns of infantry appeared moving in the same direction. The French continued their retreat on the 9th; but a strong rear-guard of about 2,000 cavalry, and several battalions of infantry, remained in sight. On the 10th, the British broke up from their position, and, while the light division, supported by the cavalry, advanced towards the Agueda, the rest of the army returned to cantonments, and the original investment of Almeida was resumed.

Colonel Trant arrived on the 7th with a division of Portuguese, and the corps of Don Julian Sanchez took a share in the action, and checked the enemy's movements on the right.

Early on the morning of the 11th the garrison of Almeida made a sortie, and cut their way to the bridge of San Felices through the British piquets, with the exception of 470, who were either killed, or wounded, and taken.

General Brenier, the governor, had previously blown up several bastions and the curtains next the Coa, and destroyed the guns of the fortress, with an immense quantity of stores in the arsenal, which was burnt. The prisoners were mostly in a state of intoxication, which was also the case with the French cavalry on the 5th instant.

Soon after daylight, General Pack, with his brigade of infantry, entered Almeida. It appears that the French evacuated the town about midnight on the 10th, and, having formed in column, waited near some ruined houses, a short distance from the walls, until the explosion took place. Their object was to destroy the *revêtement* or outer rampart, and the branches of the grand mine were conducted accordingly.

Anxious to ascertain the success of his labours, the commanding engineer remained behind, intending to follow the garrison on the Mulparteda road, but he is said to have perished in one of the chambers, owing to which circumstance the whole of the mines were not sprung. The bastions of the faces nearest the Coa were demolished, and the intervening curtain destroyed.

The stone work of the ramparts fell into the ditch, and part was carried completely over. No injury, on this occasion, was done to the town, which had suffered most severely by the explosion of the grand magazine in August last, previous to its surrender to the French. In consequence of that event, Almeida became one vast heap of ruins, a great number of the garrison and of the inhabitants perished; the southwest curtain sustained considerable damages, and few houses escaped without receiving some material injury. Of the two magazines which were placed in the castle, (the most elevated spot in Almeida,) not one stone remained upon another, nor can the foundation of these buildings be now distinguished.

The enemy had been for some days previous to the 10th, employed in spiking the guns and otherwise otherwise rendering them useless: the whole of the military stores were then collected in the arsenal and set on fire. It is here proper to remark, that the French shewed some degree of consideration for the remaining inhabitants of this devoted town, and they do not complain of any ill treatment.

The campaign, by the fall of Almeida, may now be considered at an end, as far as regards Portugal; and the whole kingdom has again been delivered from the yoke of France, whose hitherto victorious legions, under the command of their able chiefs, have, in every instance, met with disgrace and defeat when opposed to the British troops.

Appendix, R

Battle of Albuera.

Operations of Marshal Sir William Beresford on the Guadiana— Battle of Albuera— General Lumley's brilliant affair with the French Cavalry at Usagra—The Siege of Badajos raised a second time—The whole of the Allied Army in the Alentejo—Lord Wellington in the beginning of August recrosses the Tagus and invests Ciudad Rodrigo, into which Marmont throws Supplies on the 24th September, and advances over the Agueda—The Allied Army takes up a Position in front of the Coa—Marmont retires.

Pinhel, 5th December, 1811.

Previous to the commencement of Massena's retreat from Santarem, Marshals Soult and Mortier advanced from the south of Spain, in order to form a combined operation with the army of Portugal. In pursuance of this object the latter possessed himself of Merida on the 9th January, and forthwith invested Badajos with his infantry, placing his cavalry on the right bank of the Guadiana.

General Mendizabel was dispatched to the relief of Badajos on the 20th of January, with the Spanish corps, which, under the command of the Marquis de la Romana, had joined Lord Wellington in the lines, on the 19th of October. After some trifling manoeuvres, the Spanish General threw himself into the city, from whence he again withdrew his army on the 9th February, and took up a position on the ridge of St. Christoval, which commanded an extensive view in every direction. Notwithstanding this advantage, which appears to have been disregarded by General Mendizabel, the French army crossed the Gevora and Guadiana, surprised and totally defeated the Spaniards. The French cavalry pursued the fugitives (who, as usual, threw away their arms,) across the plain to the walls of Elvas, and captured the whole of the Spanish artillery and baggage.

The enemy was thus enabled to sit down quietly before Badajos; and M. Mortier lost no time in breaking ground and commencing the siege. A small breach having been made on the 10th, (but by no means practicable for assault, if properly defended,) the traitor Imaz, who succeeded to the command, on General Menacho being killed, although apprised that Marshal Beresford was marching to his relief, surrendered the city, and a garrison equal in number to the enemy. General Menacho had made every disposition for defending the place to the last extremity; the streets were barricaded, and the garrison was well supplied with ammunition and provisions for a month.

The French had previously obtained possession of Olivenza and its garrison, consisting of 3000 Spaniards; but a Portuguese force of only 250 men bravely defended the fortress of Campo Mayor from the 14th to the 21st of March. On the 25th, Marshal Beresford, having been reinforced by the Hon. Major-General Cole's division of infantry, advanced against Campo Mayor, which the enemy abandoned on the appearance of the British and Portuguese cavalry. Two squadrons of the 13th Dragoons, and two squadrons of Portuguese charged the French cavalry, who were broken and pursued to Badajos, but the infantry effected their retreat to the fortress in a solid body, although with considerable loss, and recovered the cannon which had been taken by the allied cavalry. It was unfortunate that the infantry were not combined in this operation, as the capture or destruction of the enemy would have been completely effected with their assistance.

After this affair, Sir William Beresford threw a bridge over the Guadiana at Jurumenha, and in the course of the 4th and 5th of April he crossed with his army; then leaving General Cole's division to attack Olivenza, he advanced with the whole of his remaining force, and drove the enemy (who did not think it expedient to risk an action) into the Sierra Morena. Having accomplished this object, and Olivenza having surrendered to the Hon. Major-General Cole on the 15th April, Marshal Beresford returned to undertake the siege of Badajos, which place was completely invested on the 7th of May by the allied army, and a Spanish corps commanded by Don Carlos D'Espagne. On the following day the batteries were opened against fort St. Christoval, and the garrison returned a very brisk fire upon the besiegers.

Sir William Beresford having received information on the 18th, that Marshal Soult was advancing from Seville, dispatched a courier to Lord Wellington with that intelligence; and judging it necessary to suspend his operations against Badajos, the heavy field train was sent back to Elvas. Lord Wellington lost no time in reinforcing Marshal Sir William Beresford with the 3rd and 7th divisions of infantry, under Generals Picton and Houston, and proceeded himself to Elvas, which his lordship reached on the 19th instant. Meantime, however, the battle of Albuera was fought on the heights, above the village of that name; and Marshal Soult was completely repulsed by the allied British and Portuguese Army under Sir William Beresford, and a corps of 10,000 Spaniards, commanded by Generals Blake and Castanos.

The superior numbers of the enemy's cavalry enabled him to make good his retreat towards Seville, which he commenced on the morning of the 18th, two days after the action. The Hon. General Lumley followed them with the British and Portuguese cavalry to Usagre, where the enemy, having collected a considerable force, attacked the allied cavalry on the 26th instant. Major-General Lumley had previously retired through Usagre, and having posted his troops on some favourable ground behind that village, waited the enemy's attack. Three regiments dashed through Usagre in a very resolute manner, but had scarcely formed when they were charged by General de Grey's brigade of heavy cavalry and completely overturned. The French cavalry immediately broke and fled, leaving a number of prisoners and killed and wounded on the field. The nature of the country did not permit General Lumley to follow up the advantage which he had so happily gained with a very trifling loss.

The siege of Badajos was now resumed, and on the 2nd of June batteries were re-opened against fort St. Christoval and the body of the place. A breach having been effected in fort St. Christoval, an attempt was made on the 6th of June to carry the work, and subsequently, on the night of the 9th, both of which failed, and the besiegers retired with loss. Before daybreak, on the 6th of June, the Guards once more marched from Almadilla, and passing through Aldea de Ponte, arrived about 8 a. m. at the miserable village of Robilosa, where they halted until noon. The brigade then marched by Alfayates to Soita, and bivouacked about a mile beyond.

At four in the morning of the 7th, the Guards at the head of the 1st division moved off to Sabugal, and crossing the Coa at the bridge, took up a position on the left bank of the river, and threw out strong piquets to protect the fords. In the course of the day the light division and the 6th arrived on this ground. This movement was occasioned by the enemy's having pushed forward a considerable body of cavalry and some infantry in front of Ciudad Rodrigo, on which Sir Brent

Spencer withdrew his outposts, expecting to be attacked on the 7th or 8th by the whole of the enemy's force in that quarter. These operations of the French leader, Marshal Marmont, (who had succeeded to the command of the army on Massena's recall to Paris,) appear to have been made with a view of masking his real intention; for early in the afternoon of the 8th it was ascertained that the enemy was moving in force towards the pass of Bainos. The troops were then directed to proceed to the Alentejo, and on the 14th and 15th the column crossed the Tagus at the romantic pass of the Villa Velha, over a flying bridge. Lieutenant Johnston of the Royal Artillery was unfortunately drowned while trying this ford.

On the 16th the brigade entered Portalegre, in which city the 6th and light division were also quartered, and on the 19th the 1st division marched to Assumar, and the light division to Aronches. On the 23rd the Guards advanced to St. Olaya, and halted near that town.

Previous to this period the commander of the forces had again raised the siege of Badajos, the enemy having assembled the whole of his disposable force in Estremadura, and still retaining a considerable superiority in cavalry over the British. On the 22nd the enemy advanced 40 squadrons of his cavalry and some field-pieces, for the purpose of making a reconnoissance; but although they carried off a piquet of the 11th Dragoons, commanded by Captain Lutyens, yet on the appearance of the British and Portuguese cavalry, the French retired into Badajos, without having seen the position of the allied army, the right of which rested upon Elvas, the line extending along a ridge intersected by the small River Caya, towards the fortress of Campo Mayor, in which the 7th division of the army was quartered. The main body of the allied army was in huts.

In the beginning of July, Marshal Soult, leaving from 6,000 to 7,000 men in Badajos, placed his army in cantonments, having his headquarters at Asugal; Marmont at Truxillo; and Regnier in Merida.

The British and Portuguese Army continued in camp until the 24th July; being the anniversary of the Battle of Talavera, an entertainment was given at headquarters, and a ball in the evening, which was attended by General Castanos and his suite, the officers in garrison, and some of the principal inhabitants of this city.

Marmont having passed the Tagus, and established himself at Placentia; in the beginning of August the main body of the British Army recrossed the river at Villa Velha, and the commander of the forces fixed his headquarters at Fuente Guinaldo, about two leagues from

Ciudad Rodrigo. Part of the infantry was pushed forward on the Salamanca road, and all communication cut off betwixt the fortress and the enemy.

As it was known in the early part of September that a convoy was preparing at Salamanca, destined for the relief of Ciudad Rodrigo, the combined forces were assembled on the line of the Agueda on the 23rd of that month. About 2 p. m. on the following day, the head of the convoy was observed entering the fortress, and in the course of the same night the whole arrived. For its protection, the enemy had assembled a large army, consisting of 55,000 infantry and 6,000 cavalry. Of this force General Baraguay D'Hilliers, Count D'Orsenne, brought 22,000 from Salamanca, and the remainder were the divisions under Marmont, which, since their retiring from Estremadura, had been cantoned at Placentia, Talavera de la Reyna, and other towns on the upper Tagus. Previous to the enemy's approach, the British outposts were withdrawn to the left bank of the Agueda; over which the enemy pushed his advanced guard, two regiments of cavalry and 3000 infantry, on the evening of the 24th.

Next day at noon the enemy moved a force upon the 3rd division, Major-General Picton's, which remained in a strong position on the right bank of the Azava, and the French cavalry advancing in considerable numbers, took two pieces of Portuguese artillery, after cutting down the men at their guns. The 5th regiment then charged in the most gallant style, retook these two pieces, and subsequently retired with the 77th regiment in one square, the 19th Portuguese regiment forming another, before the French cavalry, who repeatedly charged three faces of the British square without effect. This manoeuvre was directed by the Hon. Major-General Colville; and the 11th Light Dragoons, commanded by Colonel Cumming, and German hussars, succeeded in keeping the immensely superior force of the enemy in check.

About three o'clock the enemy appeared in front of Carpio, and his movements having manifested a design upon that village, a place of no importance, Major-General Alexander Campbell withdrew the 6th division behind the Duas Casas to the woods in front of Nave d'Aver.

On the 26th of September the enemy was in motion to the right. He also shewed a force in front of Fuente Guinaldo, and deployed in view of the British already drawn up in line under the immediate orders of Lord Wellington; but after some time he relinquished his intended attack, and having reformed his columns, continued his movement to the right.

At three in the morning of the 27th of September, the 1st division marched through Villa Mayor to Bismula, which they reached before noon, and at ten p.m. the troops were again in motion, and made a night march to Rondo, which they passed about four in the morning, and halted in a wood half a mile beyond. Heavy rains for some hours. In this position, the left of the ground on which the commander of the forces had determined to meet the threatened attack of the enemy, the 1st division remained until the following day, and then crossed the Coa to take up cantonments in the valley of the Mondego; and thus ended the active part of the campaign of 1811.

General Graham's Orders.

Rondo, 28th Sept. 1811.

The Lieutenant-General has received the orders of His Excellency the commander of the forces, to march the troops into cantonments, as the enemy has abandoned the attempt of attacking the army in this position. He is confident that the left could not have been forced, defended by such troops as he has the honour to command.

LEONAUR

ALSO FROM LEONAUR
AVAILABLE IN SOFTCOVER OR HARDCOVER WITH DUST JACKET

OFFICERS & GENTLEMEN *by Peter Hawker & William Graham*—Two Accounts of British Officers During the Peninsula War: Officer of Light Dragoons by Peter Hawker & Campaign in Portugal and Spain by William Graham .

THE WALCHEREN EXPEDITION *by Anonymous*—The Experiences of a British Officer of the 81st Regt. During the Campaign in the Low Countries of 1809.

LADIES OF WATERLOO *by Charlotte A. Eaton, Magdalene de Lancey & Juana Smith*—The Experiences of Three Women During the Campaign of 1815: Waterloo Days by Charlotte A. Eaton, A Week at Waterloo by Magdalene de Lancey & Juana's Story by Juana Smith.

JOURNAL OF AN OFFICER IN THE KING'S GERMAN LEGION *by John Frederick Hering*—Recollections of Campaigning During the Napoleonic Wars.

JOURNAL OF AN ARMY SURGEON IN THE PENINSULAR WAR *by Charles Boutflower*—The Recollections of a British Army Medical Man on Campaign During the Napoleonic Wars.

ON CAMPAIGN WITH MOORE AND WELLINGTON *by Anthony Hamilton*—The Experiences of a Soldier of the 43rd Regiment During the Peninsular War.

THE ROAD TO AUSTERLITZ *by R. G. Burton*—Napoleon's Campaign of 1805.

SOLDIERS OF NAPOLEON *by A. J. Doisy De Villargennes & Arthur Chuquet*—The Experiences of the Men of the French First Empire: Under the Eagles by A. J. Doisy De Villargennes & Voices of 1812 by Arthur Chuquet .

INVASION OF FRANCE, 1814 *by F. W. O. Maycock*—The Final Battles of the Napoleonic First Empire.

LEIPZIG—A CONFLICT OF TITANS *by Frederic Shoberl*—A Personal Experience of the 'Battle of the Nations' During the Napoleonic Wars, October 14th-19th, 1813.

SLASHERS *by Charles Cadell*—The Campaigns of the 28th Regiment of Foot During the Napoleonic Wars by a Serving Officer.

BATTLE IMPERIAL *by Charles William Vane*—The Campaigns in Germany & France for the Defeat of Napoleon 1813-1814.

SWIFT & BOLD *by Gibbes Rigaud*—The 60th Rifles During the Peninsula War.

AVAILABLE ONLINE AT **www.leonaur.com**
AND FROM ALL GOOD BOOK STORES
07/09

Lightning Source UK Ltd.
Milton Keynes UK
UKHW011831091019

351318UK00001B/21/P